EARLY CHURCH ART
IN NORTHERN EUROPE

Half-timber Church at Besford, Worcestershire.

Sidney Pitcher, Gloucester, *photo.*

EARLY CHURCH ART
IN NORTHERN EUROPE

WITH SPECIAL REFERENCE TO
TIMBER CONSTRUCTION AND DECORATION

By

JOSEF STRZYGOWSKI

HACKER ART BOOKS
New York
1980

Based on lectures delivered before the
University of London at University College

First Published London, 1928
Reissued 1980 by Hacker Art Books, New York

Library of Congress Catalogue Card Number 77-73725
International Standard Book Number 0-87817-246-7

Printed in the United States of America.

To

THE VICE-CHANCELLOR OF THE

UNIVERSITY OF LONDON

ERNEST A. GARDNER

PREFACE

SOME difficulty has been experienced in suitably representing in the illustrations a number of churches and other monuments referred to in the text situated in obscure parts of Europe and in many cases never before illustrated except in the Transactions of Learned Societies and other publications of Central European origin. Most of such sources are noted in the text when they occur, but the Author would like here to express his general obligation for the facilities which have been afforded him to reproduce these subjects, without which the task of illustrating the book would have been rendered considerably more difficult.

For the fine series of illustrations of Norwegian churches (Plates XXXIX.-XLIII. inclusive) he is indebted to Mr. Martin Olsson. The subjects on Plates XXIV. (*a*), XXVII. (*a*), XXVIII. (*a*) and XXXV. are from photographs by Mr. Herbert Felton, F.R.P.S.; those on Plates XXV., XXVII. and XXX. (*a*) by Mr. F. H. Crossley, F.S.A., of Chester; those on Plate XXVI. by Dr. G. Granville Buckley, F.S.A.; that on Plate XXXII. (*b*) by Messrs. F. Frith & Co., of Reigate; and those on Plate XXXVIII. by Mr. Arthur Gardner, to all of whom the Author would like to express his indebtedness for their inclusion.

On account of the differences in the construction treated in this book from the ordinary English methods of building, it has been thought advisable to adopt the following nomenclature in regard to the various forms of building in timber :—

(*a*) SOLID TIMBER CONSTRUCTION.—This is generally described as *Blockwork* throughout the text, and denotes building with logs placed close together.

(*b*) HALF-TIMBER CONSTRUCTION.—In speaking of English work this term has generally been employed, but to make the method of construction apparent it has been referred to sometimes in other chapters as *Framework*.

(*c*) FULL TIMBER CONSTRUCTION.—This term is sometimes used in contradistinction to Half-Timber Construction. The type of work denoted is similar to Blockwork, but naturally with variations in construction owing to building at different times and in different places.

(*d*) STAVE WORK.—This term is used for the Mast Type of Timber construction found in the Norwegian churches described in Chapter IV.

CONTENTS

INTRODUCTION

THE purpose of the present volume is to summarize some books written by me in 1916 and subsequent years based on researches in Northern Europe. The international situation made it impossible for me to return to Asia, and this, together with the trend of my archæological convictions, led me to the North.

For about thirty years I worked along the lines suggested by such catch-phrases as " Orient or Rome ? " " Orient or Byzantium ? " " Altai-Iran and the Migrations." A résumé of this part of my work is given in my *Origin of Christian Church Art* (Oxford, 1923), consisting of eight lectures delivered first at the University of Upsala in Sweden, and later, in 1922, at the Lowell Institute at Boston, Mass. My studies in the Asiatic field were published in a number of large works, *Asia Minor, a New Country for the History of Art*, *Mschatta*, *Amida*, and others. Meanwhile conditions have changed, and it is clear to me that I cannot continue indefinitely producing books of monumental size which stand no chance of being printed : first I must produce my results in the hope that some institution or publisher may thus be emboldened to publish my books of elaborate scientific investigations.

What I wish to demonstrate as a result of my work, which extends over more than the last ten years, is that the history of mediæval art rests on an unsound foundation if it looks for its origin only to Greek and Roman, Early Christian, and Italian art. There existed a North European art about which we are ignorant, since the monuments were chiefly of wood, and have consequently not survived. There are, however, traces of these which may serve as a starting-point for our studies. I shall draw attention to four landmarks of mediæval wood architecture beginning with the Slav movement towards the South, and the Northern hinterland in the east of Europe. Thus we shall become acquainted with construction of beams placed together horizontally. In the third lecture we come to the cultural zone which also includes the British

I

Isles, the zone of half-timber work.   But the North Sea had a wholly different system of wood architecture, which we see in the fourth chapter, in the Norwegian " mast-churches." We shall inquire into the origin of this art, concluding, in the fifth chapter, with shipbuilding.   At the same time we shall consider the decoration on the monuments, and discuss the question of early European ornament, its essential character and evolution.

I may have some difficulty in carrying conviction with the facts and theories which will be given prominence in these lectures.   We are all, here and in America, proud of our European origin, using the term Europe in the cultural sense to denote the influence of Greece and Rome and the effect of the humanistic movement working in two directions (pagan and Christian) on our knowledge and culture.   My own point of view is somewhat different.   I am not inclined to place the study of Greece and Rome before that of the North.   I believe that we should divest ourselves of the influence of humanism and begin to see with our own, that is, with northern eyes.   As is usually found, we can write history and formulate principles, in the manner of Chinese Confucianism, along the lines of our humanistic ancestors. But the time comes when we ask for more.   We wish to know not only what has been, but what is, and what shall be : what values have existed from the beginning till now, and from what influences these have been derived.   Having found that, our experience and knowledge may bear fruit directly not only in the sciences but in culture and art, in our own lives and the future.   Our work is no longer concerned only with the past : we begin to feel that archæology pursued for its own sake is wasted time, Europe is something more than what humanistic teaching represented : and we shall best appreciate it, if we first of all know our own North.   My lectures deal with architecture and ornament in Europe before the South, that is Rome and Byzantium, moved northwards ; and perhaps we shall find that what we can see with our eyes in art may be present in other departments of culture.

*　　*　　*　　*　　*　　*　　*　　*　　*

It is now three years since this book was written, and I feel the necessity for adding a few words on the nature of my work during the intervening period.   My book dealing with the position taken by Finland in the history of the world's art has not yet been printed. In the meanwhile I have spent the major part of my time in researches on Asiatic art as a whole (see my book *Wesen und Entwicklung der bildenden Kunst in Asien*), and in work on a book on mankind in general from deductions gathered during a life of research on the Fine Arts (*Der sächliche Aufbau des Menschentums und die Entwicklung der Menschheit von der bildenden Kunst ausgesehen*). None of these books was written in the expectation of immediate publication, for the present does not seem to me a suitable time to treat of such questions. I have therefore taken the opportunity of dealing very briefly with a few of the points that occur in the present Introduction.

The chapters that comprise this book (originally delivered as lectures) are all written along an underlying theory which I first formulated in my book *Die Krisis der Geisteswissenschaften* (1923). I have attempted throughout to distinguish systematically between actual knowledge of the monuments dealt with and their sources, and their essential character and evolutionary significance. I deal critically with such monuments as they appear to me as a result of the methodical research I have employed in their investigation.

This book does not follow on the usual lines of art-histories as they have been written from the time of the Renaissance onwards. The principal concern of these in our particular province is with stone buildings, chiefly churches, and the naturalistic representation of the human figure. This, one is told, is high art—a field worthy of the efforts of the cultivated connoisseur. I question very much whether this is a scientific attitude. Following Vasari and his predecessors in the same tradition, we are apt to consider every art not in the direct line of stone construction and naturalistic representation a primitive one, and the peoples practising it barbarians. We fail to observe that at one time the greater part of the world was averse to such principles, as at the present day is the entire art of Islam. We form our observations from study of the art of the Mediterranean countries and lands of similar climate between the Alps, the Taurus, and the Himalayas, that is, speaking roughly, the Tropic of Cancer, which I call the Intermediate Zone between the extremes of North and South. It is a doubtful question whether this middle zone possesses an artistic identity of its own, or whether it is merely composed of elements drawn from the zones of North and South.

The new outlook in art-history draws a clear distinction between these three zones, and emphasizes the contrast between the Northern and Southern extremes. From the traditional point of view the North and South in Europe itself are clearly differentiated, but it is necessary to reckon with the fact that actually no part of Europe, or, for that matter, of Asia belongs properly to the geographical South, lands in Europe and Asia which we designate loosely as " Southern " belonging as a matter of fact to the Intermediate or Middle Zone.   The boundary of the geographical South lies along the Equator.

It is not difficult to realize the enormous influence which the difference between the cold of the geographical North and the heat of the geographical South has exercised in the development of humanity. Formerly in the study of art it was only the middle zone and, more especially, the Mediterranean area that was found worthy of attention. Now, if we begin to consider the world as a whole, we can see how totally the aspect changes.

At one extreme is the equatorial South, at the other the North around the Pole.   The principal concern of the latter is with the building of strong shelters against the weather, and the adequate clothing of the body against the cold—both unnecessary in the tropical South.   As a consequence it is obviously in the North that handicrafts develop most freely and flourish most liberally.

In the present work it is the North with which we are concerned.   It seems only logical that if I devote much attention to the North of Europe I should also, if only in this Introduction, make some mention of the *Asiatic* North beside.   It is here that Siberia attains a new significance, to which I drew insufficient attention in some of my earlier works. I believe that in speaking of Nearer Asia (that is to say, excluding Hither Asia and India) from the point of view of art, we have not only to reckon with West Asia (Iran), the Turkish (now Mongolian) Centre, and East Asia, but also with a continuous art-stream from the North that once possessed an individual character of its own.   It is difficult to speak of this art, because, as we shall see in the case of Europe, its principal raw materials have vanished, as, for example, the leather work of Siberia.   All that have come down to us are the remains of objects in gold, silver, bronze, and various stones.   We can find, however, numerous affinities between North Asiatic

and North European art, as, for instance, in the making
of parchment and parchment decoration. Though at the
present time our knowledge of this North Asiatic art amounts
to very little, yet it is beginning more and more to claim our
attention. Later, Iran becomes the predominating source
on which Siberian art draws, while at the same time another
stream of Turkish influence makes steady encroachments.
Certain indications that may be gathered from America
and, later, from the Mongolian expansion give rise to hypo-
theses with which I shall not deal at the moment. These
are briefly touched upon in the pages that follow. I do
not, however, share the opinion of Minns that Siberian art
depends largely on a connection with Greece, nor that of
Rostovtzeff who makes it directly dependent on Iran. I
merely repeat what I have already hinted, that traces are to be
found indicating that Siberia once possessed a flourishing and
characteristic art proper to itself.

I trust that it will by now be almost unnecessary for me
to lay any further stress on the importance of the Turkish and
Iranian influence in the development of art. I have already
shown in my books on Mschatta, Armenia, and Alt-Iran,
how the art of Turkish Upper Asia developed from the tent
and a certain form of metal-work, and that of Western Asia
(Iran) from the use of unburnt brick and wall-casing. My
new book on Asia deals with each of these art-streams, comparing them systematically and drawing further conclusions,
rather as Mr. O. M. Dalton has done in his recent work, *East
Christian Art*, which is not only, as the author modestly desig-
nates it, "a survey of the monuments," but also a serious
and masterly investigation of a number of the problems propounded by myself in earlier works.

I am indebted to Mr. Alec B. Tonnochy, of the British
Museum, for the reading, revision, and, where necessary, re-
writing of my English manuscript. I have myself read the
printed proofs.

JOSEF STRZYGOWSKI.

VIENNA, *October*, 1928.

CHAPTER I.

THE PRE-ROMANESQUE ART OF THE CROATIANS.

THE question is never asked whether the Slav peoples had any part in or influence upon the development of early European art : it is generally assumed that they had not. In all histories of art on a large or on a small scale, ancient art is followed by the Early Christian art of the Mediterranean countries ; thence by some means they proceed to mediæval art, ignoring the possibility that Slav or East European art had a place in its evolution ; they do not even inquire into the possible existence of monuments in Eastern Europe which might have some bearing on the transition from ancient to mediæval art.

By this expression, the transition from ancient to mediæval art, we understand a dark age in which any light we can throw upon the period is welcome. We have been so accustomed to look at the matter from the Roman or Byzantine point of view, that it was only after more than thirty years' work that I succeeded in pointing to the probability of an Eastern influence, that is to say, an influence from the Eastern North and Central Asia. In this first chapter I shall try to study this question in so far as it relates to the European East only. Is there no sign-post on the road which we have failed to observe ?

This chapter, as its title shows, deals with the pre-Romanesque art of the Croatians. In vain do we look for it in the handbooks of art-history : we apparently cannot conceive that barbarians, that is to say, destructive, not constructive forces, should be accepted by a tribunal in which the adherents of Rome and Byzantium sit in judgment and pass criticism on art, even though in course of time works of art hitherto ignored sue for recognition. The position is always the same : we are chained by our humanistic education to the South : Rome, and, for the East, Byzantium, are the centres from which the barbarian North received its entire culture. To take an example, the earliest West Slav buildings preserved near Prague and in Moravia are round stone churches : at once we produce literary evidence to the effect that a pupil of the Slav apostle, Methodius, the priest Kaich, together with Prince Borivoy, eight years after his baptism, built the Church of St. Clement on the Levy Hradec ; Methodius came from Byzantium, therefore the early Bohemian churches must be of Byzantine origin.   In the same way it is demonstrated *a priori* that all longitudinal churches must be of Roman or Romanesque origin.   I showed in a paper published in the journal *Slavia*, III. (1924), that it was not only possible but probable that the round church is not a peculiarly Byzantine form, but one which also appears independently in the North built with rag-stone, and that longitudinal churches are often built on the square plan, a sure indication of a non-Roman origin.

Another example of this point is found in the views expressed on the finest of the Hiberno-Saxon monuments, the crosses of Ruthwell in Dumfriesshire and especially that of Bewcastle, which I visited, and which is still in its original position in the Cheviots.   The humanist declares that they cannot be earlier than Romanesque monuments of the same kind, and that they date from the eleventh century.   But the student of the North and its relations with the Far East replies that this art was possible in the seventh century.   May I refer my readers to my *Origin of Christian Church Art*, where especially the necessity for a new horizon for the historian of mediæval art is discussed ?   As I had in that book the question of Hither Asia and its relation to Europe in my mind, so it is my purpose in these chapters to show that the European East and the Scandinavian North have to be treated independently, and that, here too, the Roman and Byzantine prejudice prevents all unbiassed research and precludes the possibility of escape from the blind alley in which the art-history of the dark ages, from the seventh to the eleventh century, is imprisoned.

As with the Ruthwell and Bewcastle crosses, so opinions differ on the dating of pre-Romanesque churches in Spain. A good many of them can be attributed from inscriptions and artistic features to the seventh and eighth centuries, before the Mohammedan conquest in the year 711.   The most significant fact about these buildings is that they are barrel- or cupola-vaulted, and that the arch is not the usual round arch but of horse-shoe shape.   I was able to point out in my *Amida*, 1910, that those vaulted churches show striking analogies with Mesopotamian types, especially those of the monasteries in the Tur Abdin. In 1914 Rivoira, well known as a champion of the principle, " All roads lead to Rome," published a book, *Architettura musulmana*, in which he undertook to prove that the Visigothic churches all belonged to a later period, and that, for example, the horse-shoe arch was introduced into Spain only by the Mohammedans. I mention this point because a pupil of Rivoira made the same attempt with regard to some of the oldest and most interesting Croatian churches and church-types of Dalmatia : they were all demonstrably of the eleventh century, not pre-Romanesque, because in Italy such churches were certainly not earlier than that. How was it possible, argues Rivoira, that the early North-European art should penetrate to the peninsulas of the south, and produce Christian monuments earlier than those of Italy ?

What is early North European church art ? The British Isles are fortunate in being able to answer the question. So splendid are the Irish and Anglo-Saxon monuments that in Scandinavia scholars are led to believe that the germ of their own Christian art must have come from these islands. In France, Germany, and Switzerland the names of the great missionaries are as well known as they are at home. There perhaps more than in Scandinavia is the influence of Irish and Anglo-Saxon art apparent. I shall not touch on those familiar subjects in the present chapter. Western Europe lies outside the horizon, although I shall constantly refer to the countries in which originated the principal mediæval styles, which in time overflowed over all the countries of Europe, as far as the Roman faith extended.

I propose here to deal only with the marginal countries of Western Europe, the Teutonic far north and the Slavonic east. There was originally an essential difference between the three art-streams, the West European, the Scandinavian, and the Slavonic. This disappeared later with the supremacy of the Romanesque style. What we call to-day Western Europe is Roman Catholic Europe, to which belong also the Slavonic Catholics, the Scandinavians, and the Finnish Protestants. Now when we come to the pre-Romanesque architecture of Europe, the difference will at once be apparent : they built altogether in wood, but Western Europe built in framework, the East in beam or blockwork and the North in stave-work. In the second, third, and fourth chapters we shall say more about block, frame, and stave or mast-work.

The first chapter only prepares the field, the last opens the door to pre-Christian times.   It will become evident that during the dark ages we are not at the beginning but at the end of a flourishing northern art.

Northern Europe did not lag behind that other extremity of the northern world, China.   In that country the first thousand years of our era marked a period of the highest artistic culture.   Hitherto we have supposed that this was a time of artistic deadness in European art.   This, however, is a mistaken view.   As in China the thousand years before Christ saw a purely northern or non-representational art, so did the first thousand years A.D. in Europe.   Southern art with its representational character and human figure-subjects began in China shortly before the introduction of Buddhism about the time of the birth of Christ : the same movement began in the North of Europe a thousand years later, when the Roman or Byzantine church developed its missionary work on the Continent, in Scandinavia, and in the Slavonic countries.   Until then the representation of the human figure was exceptional. Of the tendencies in architecture we are ignorant both as regards Europe and Asia.   It may be that in both of the northern countries a perishable material was used, the monuments in which have disappeared.   It is, however, possible to reconstruct this lost architecture.   In the present work I shall attempt to do this for the North of Europe.   This Northern Europe penetrated to the South, especially to the peninsular countries.   We find the Western Goths in Spain, the Eastern Goths and the Lombards in Italy, and the Croats and Serbians, as once the Greeks, in the Balkans.   I speak in the title of early North European art: by beginning in my first chapter with the Croatians I indicate that Croatian art is a part of the early North European movement, notwithstanding that the monuments are found in the South, on the Adriatic coast of the Mediterranean.

The Croatians inhabit the country from the bend of the Danube near Belgrade between the Drave and the Save (Slavonia) to the Adriatic coast south of Reka (Fiume), Croatia proper, and the long strip along the Adriatic coast in Dalmatia.   Bosnia, in the angle between Croatia and Dalmatia, has a mixed population of Croats and Serbians.   These two Slavonic peoples are distinguished not only by their languages but by their church, the Croats being Catholics, while the Serbians belong to the Orthodox Church.

I. Study of the Monuments.—The pre-Romanesque art
of the Croatians falls into two divisions: architectural
monuments on the one hand, and decorative sculpture on the
other.   When I first visited the east coast of the Adriatic in
1887, I found in all parts of Zadar stone fragments, some of
which are preserved in the Museum, small pieces of stone
with interlaced band ornament, which were of interest to me
as I had seen similar examples in 1883 in England, and in 1885
in all parts of Italy from the north down to as far as Rome.
I brought away some photographs, but at that time I took
little interest in the small churches and ruins where such
ornaments exist or have been found.   To-day, after nearly
forty years, this church building is, in my view, of the first
importance: and it is remarkable that only by some such
small fragments of interlaced ornament can we tell that a
Croatian church once existed in a certain spot, or that the ruins
belonged to early Croatian times because that ornament had
been found there.   For it must be remembered that the number
of these decorated pieces is infinitely greater than the buildings
themselves to which they belonged.   There is no single
Croatian church extant which is not in ruins, to show the
original plan of the building and the liturgical furniture as it
stood.   They have all been destroyed or restored, and we
can point out one fact only which is of some value, namely,
that there was no rich decoration on the church buildings
themselves, outside or inside, on the walls or on the roof;
only the church furniture shows an abundance of ornament.
In the churches that remain it was of stone.

My first impression of the early Croatian monuments, in
1887, is characteristic: the churches were small, dirty, and
neglected, the decorated fragments lying about equally
neglected: the people were apathetic about them, and there
was no attempt at classification or arrangement.   On my last
visit to Croatia and Dalmatia in March and April, 1924,
the situation was not much better.   We may hope, however,
that with the constitution of the national Yugo-Slav state,
the people of the various countries will acquire a keen interest
in their own monuments, and that the time is not far off when
we shall contemplate not only the buildings of Greek and
Roman times—in Dalmatia, for example, the palace of Dio-
cletian at Spalato, and the great churches of the Early Christian,
Romanesque, Gothic, and Renaissance periods—but also
the more modest remains of the first centuries after the Yugo-

Slav emigration down to 1105, when Croatia became a part of Hungary.

A good many of the Croatian churches and ornaments are dated by inscriptions. There is, for instance, in the Museum at Zagreb a stone which not only has the name of King

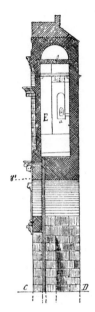

FIG. 1.—Door to Chapel, Porta Aurea, Spalato (Split).

FIG. 2.—Porta Aurea, Spalato. Section of Wall Showing Interior Gallery.

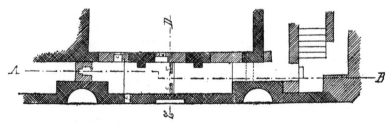

FIG. 3.—Porta Aurea, Spalato. Plan of Chapel of St. Martin.

Branimir (879-892) but the date, 888 (Plate VI. (*a*)). It is quite exceptional to find such a specific date : on other stones we find only the name of the founder, a Croatian Zupan, duke or king, a bishop, etc. It appears that all the stone furniture of the churches bore such inscriptions, and perhaps the stone churches themselves. Later I shall show as a good example of the normal dimensions of an early Croatian Church the chapel of St. Martin in the *porta aurea* of Split (Spalato), which is not itself a Croatian building, but a pagan edifice used as a Christian church which measures only 10·08 m. long by 1·63 m. broad (Figs. 1-3). The interior gallery running round the walls of the palace passes under a barrel vault above the door. The first inscription is over the west entrance to the chapel, the second being on the screen (Plate I. (*b*)) which divides this miniature church into two parts. In the same manner in several other churches built for the early Croatian dukes, names are to be found on the door or on separate parts of the church, the altar, the baptistery, or the pulpit. It seems that our best hope of dating early Croatian monuments is the discovery of a number of such inscriptions, even if these are small and fragmentary. In one place we know only of a dated fragment of the stone furniture, in another, an inscription in the church itself. The collection and systematic classification of this material will be a considerable achievement. For the purposes of the present chapter it may suffice to say that we have a possible foundation based on solid documentary and historical evidence.

To be strictly methodical, I ought to give the list of places and a description of the monuments which concern us. That is not practicable for the present purpose. We must be content with a map (Fig. 4) in which these places are shown.

I divide the subject into buildings and ornament. The buildings have been preserved only along the Adriatic littoral and the mountains extending along the coast. Beyond the Dalmatian mountains in Croatia, Slavonia, and Bosnia decorated pieces have hitherto been found in a few places only. This does not mean that there were no churches there; simply that in the first place Croatia has not been much excavated, and secondly, that stone churches could be found only on the coast, churches further inland being built originally of the more perishable wood. We are still at the initial stage in this field of research, and I hope to raise some questions in this chapter which may induce scholars to make the necessary excavations. Their work should begin in those parts of the Croatian " Mesopotamia " between the Drave and the Save where examples of interlaced band ornament have been found in Sissac, Ilok, and Rakovać. In Dalmatia two societies were engaged in excavations while the country was under Austria, and in 1885, during digging operations for the railway near Knin, an astonishing number of decorated fragments was discovered. The first society, " Bihać," for the excavation of ancient Slav monuments, was founded in 1894 at Split, confining itself to the early Croatian period, and the other, " Hrvatsko starinarsko družtva," in 1895 in Knin itself, the one working in the South, and the other in the North of Dalmatia. Their discoveries, published in their reports, were brought to the Museums of Split and Knin. We have, at present, therefore, three public collections of early Croatian

FIG. 4.—MAP OF THE DALMATIAN COAST.

monuments ; the first and richest being at Zadar (Director Bersa), now in Italian possession, the second in Split, unfortunately combined with the Museum of Roman Antiquities (Director Abramic Bulić), and the third, known as " The First Early Croatian Museum," in Knin (Director Marun). If we visualize a collection similar to that of the Anglo-Saxon and Irish crosses in the Cathedral Library at Durham, but considerably richer, we shall have some idea of the Museum at Knin, a place which was a capital in early Croatian times, situated on the point where the Kerka leaves the mountains.

We may hope that the Croatians, one of three Yugo-Slav nations equally qualified to do so, will reorganize this unique collection: especially as there is ample room in the Castle of Knin. This Museum has, moreover, given some good specimens of early Croatian ornament to the Museum at Zagreb, where they are preserved along with those mentioned above, which were found in Croatia itself. The treasures in these museums convince us to our astonishment that there was an art in early Croatia flourishing to such an extent that it cannot be explained *a priori* by the influence of another country or of a foreign (not Yugo-Slav) art-stream: it must have been indigenous to the Yugo-Slavians themselves, and produced by them from their own artistic sense. In putting forward this theory I depend only on my own researches, since scholars hitherto, and even the Croatians, or Yugo-Slavians themselves, have, I think, been misled by the old humanistic hypothesis, one section considering this art to be part of the Mediterranean tradition, another that it is Italian, the third claiming for it a Byzantine origin. These opinions cannot be critically examined in the present series of chapters, but I hope to investigate them in a subsequent book (*Researches on the Evolution of Ancient Yugo-Slavian Art*), and see if the study of the essential character and evolution of this art will not enable me to come to some definite conclusion.

There is an English work in three volumes, *Dalmatia, the Quarnero and Istria*, published in 1887, which is still of service. Its author, T. G. Jackson, was not, it is true, the pioneer: already, in 1862, Eitelberger, Professor of Art History at Vienna, was in the field. Jackson, however, was an architect, and his plans and designs are in many cases, like others of Eitelberger, the only good reproductions I have been able to find. Of the first importance, too, is the journal, *Starohrvatska Prosvjeta*, published by the Knin Archæological Society and edited by Frano Radić, a teacher of Kurciola. A new series of this journal was begun in 1927. During the years 1896-1904 Radić did his best according to his lights, but although he used the term early Croatian, he was convinced that Dalmatian art of the Knin Period was an off-shoot of Byzantine. It is to his credit that these eight volumes contain what are the first photographic reproductions of the monuments, and are, therefore, of some value still. Knin, which has been passed over by Eitelberger and Jackson, was first published by F. Bulić, *Hrvatski spomenici u Kninskoj okolici*, Zagreb, 1888:

in this work the ornament is reproduced by means of line drawings.[1]

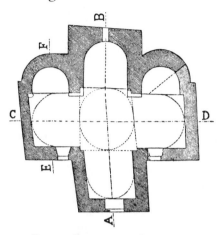

FIG, 5.—PLAN OF THE CHURCH OF S. KRIZ AT NIN.

A. *Architecture.*— The three most important sites of early Croatian (or better, Yugo-Slavian) buildings are Nin (Nona), north of Zadar (Zara), Knin, and the surroundings of Split (Spalato), and Solin (Salona). But early Croatian monuments continue southwards to Dubrovnik (Ragusa) and Kotor (Cattaro), with the islands along the Dalmatian coast which make this section of the Adriatic a region apart, like the Scandinavian and Finnish coast of the North and Baltic Seas. It is quite possible that shipbuilding was not without its effect on other types of architecture, as we shall find later, when we come to Scandinavia and Finland.

Nin, which is furthest to the north, and was the stronghold of the

[1] Here I should like to plead for the continuation by a staff of young and scholarly assistants, of the untiring field-work,' lasting for forty years, of Fra Luigi Marun, whose name is almost synonymous with Knin. The Croatian Pompeii deserves serious study and careful preservation not from the Croatians and Yugo-Slavians only, but from all interested

FIG. 6.—SECTION OF THE CHURCH OF S. KRIZ AT NIN.

in the history of northern art. Almost all the Christian remains found here are the products of northern art, having been brought to the south in the course of the Teutonic and Slav migrations.

Slavonic church in its controversies with the church of Rome, is largely in ruins. I show merely the state church S. Kriz (the Church of the Holy Cross) and S. Nicola. They are both domed churches of the Greek-cross type built on a very small scale. S. Kriz, built between 700 and 800, has an open square bay with four rectangular arms measuring 3·60 m. longitudinally, the whole being 9 by 9·20 m. (Fig. 5, Plate II. (*a*)). Over the central square there is a round tower-like cupola without windows but with blind arcades outside, as also on the gables of the four arms. The main apse is circular outside, the side apses semi-circular. Windows are found only in the west wall. The transition from the square bay to the round cupola, and from the square arms to the barrel vault is effected by squinches (*trompes*) (Fig. 6). This feature is also to be seen perfectly

FIG. 7.—CHURCH OF S. NICOLA AT NIN.

in S. Nicola of Nin (Figs. 7 and 8). The square central bay of S. Kriz under the tower opens on three horseshoe apses. On the fourth side is a rectangular bay with a vault in the form of a semi-dome supported on squinches. The apses, which are 2·0 by 1·40 m., are separated by pillars 0·44 m. in diameter in the four corners which are connected by four

FIG. 8.—SECTION OF THE CHURCH OF S. NICOLA AT NIN.

PLATE I

(a) Interior of the Church of S. Donato at Zadar (Zara) (Dalmatia)

(b) Carved stone screen in the Chapel, Porta Aurea, Spalato (Dalmatia)

PLATE II

(a) Nin. Exterior of the Church of S. Kriz

(b) Church of S .Donato at Zadar

intersecting ribs in the ceiling. Consequently, here, too, the cupola has no windows. We shall see a similar principle of construction in the wooden churches of Finland.

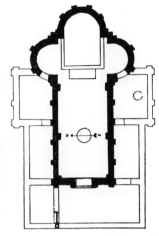

A church of a kindred type to S. Nicola of Nin is found south of Sibenik (Sebenico) in Bilice. It has three round apses, and on the fourth side of the square bay a long nave (Fig. 9). Some decorated work of great interest has been found in this church. In Zadar there was at one time a church, S. Vito, of a similar type to S. Kriz. The most famous church in that town is the church of S. Donato. It is of quite another type, not square but round, the simplest form of which I shall

FIG. 9.—PLAN OF CHURCH NEAR SIBENIK (BILICE).

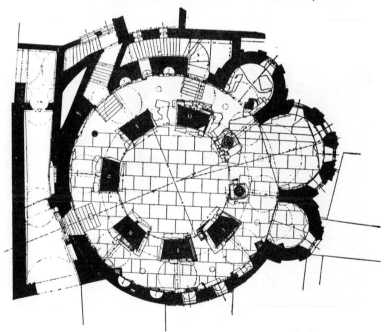

FIG. 10.—PLAN OF THE CHURCH OF S. DONATO AT ZADAR.

show later, illustrating its essential character, the round cupola on round walls. In S. Donato the cupola lies not on the outer, but on an inner wall pierced by eight high and narrow arches (Fig. 10, Plate I. (*a*)). Two of the dividing

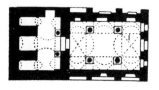

pillars, composed of huge granite columns, lead to three horse-shoe apses. The inner circle supports a high conical cupola with small windows ending in a round arch of tiles corresponding in breadth to the lower part. The nave round the cupola is barrel-vaulted and spanned by a binding arch. In the walls out-

FIG. 11.—PLAN OF THE CHURCH OF S. LORENZO AT ZADAR.

side and inside may be seen blind arcades along the walls (Plate II. (*b*)). On the north side a staircase leads to the upper storey and a round gallery with three apses. On the south side, on the upper floor, the wall opens into an adjoining room through columns. This upper church may have belonged to a private house. In S. Donato no ornaments have survived except the arch over the doorway leading to the stair-case, which shows the guilloche beloved of early Croatian art. Zadar shows also a third type of early Croatian church with a central cupola. These churches, however, have the appearance of long churches with three aisles separated by two pairs of columns. There is S. Lorenzo in Zadar (Fig. 11) : but as that is not in a good state of preservation we shall do better to turn to Split, in which the church of S. Nicola (Fig. 12), though in a state of neglect and disorder, shows the type more clearly. We see that the centre of the church is square : four columns taken from older monuments, some with early Croatian capitals, of which the most interesting example is in S. Lorenzo at Zadar, support a miniature cupola of 1·60 m., now, unfortunately, destroyed. But from the very curious vaults over the small naves we can see the construction. It is identical with that of the vaults of S. Kriz and the vestibule of S. Nicola at Nin, and the apse of S. Pietro Vecchio at Zadar (Fig.

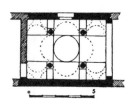

FIG. 12.—PLAN OF THE CHURCH OF S. NICOLA AT SPALATO (SPLIT).

13) ; on both sides are two rectangular compartments between the columns and the walls, every half-square having a semi-dome resting on squinches and but-tressing the barrel vault in the middle, which runs from east and west to the cupola, at right angles to a shorter barrel vault running from north to south be-tween the corner apses with the half squinch cupola.

Now this four-column type appears in several places elongated by an extra pair of columns at the west end. The best example, S. Eufemia in Split, now in ruins, has fortunately been published by Eitelberger (Fig. 14). We see here the four columns supporting the characteristic conical cupola without windows, having the appearance of a tower on the outside. The western end is elongated by two columns, but the barrel vault has no division. A very similar church was S. Domenica at Zadar, now also destroyed. It was of special

FIG. 13.—INTERIOR OF THE CHURCH OF S. PIETRO VECCHIO
AT ZADAR.

interest on account of the rich ornament found inside, especially on the building itself. Another highly interesting monument of this type is S. Barbara of Trogir (Traù) (Plate III. (*b*)), a true basilica with three aisles ; but, as in other churches, the cupola has not survived. From the form of the square apse we may reconstruct the cupola, which rested on squinches. Over the door is an inscription with the name of Maius, a prior of the city, not earlier than the eleventh century, stating that he was the founder.

The laſt cupola-type of the early Croatian ſtone churches is rather more charaĉteriſtic of Southern Dalmatia : it can be called the cupola-hall. In Kotor (Cattaro) there are two churches of this type, both without the original ceiling and roof. S. Marija (Fig. 15) was rebuilt in 1220, on the earlier plan, according to Jackson, of the original small church of about 809: there is one aisle divided into three parts by arches ; in the centre, the cupola ; at the eaſt end a groined vault ; at the weſt a barrel vault. The other church S. Luke (Fig. 16), a tiny ſtruĉture in a dirty

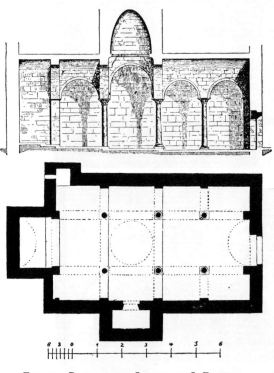

FIG. 14.—PLAN OF THE CHURCH OF S. EUFEMIA AT SPALATO (SPLIT). (AFTER EITELBERGER.)

and negleĉted condition, shows the cupola between two barrel vaults. Another example of intereſt is S. Nicola of Selaĉ on the island of Braĉ (Brazza). This church originates the type of Serbian brick architeĉture.

A good illuſtration of this type is also the church of S. Petear in Priko on the Cetina river near the coaſt (Plate III. (a)), not far from Split. The single aisle is divided by pilaſters inlaid with antique marble slabs ; it is in three parts composed of a cupola between two transverse arches. I think it probable that in early times there were barrel vaults conſtruĉted on the Mesopotamian plan, bricks laid in four triangles to the square, as in the old church of S. Sophia in the Bulgarian residence. Possibly a more detailed examination, particularly of all the purely barrel-vaulted buildings which I deal with together in the laſt group may give us data enabling us to decide this intereſting point.

PLATE III

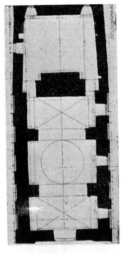

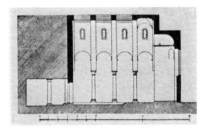

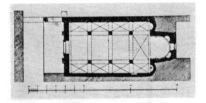

(a) Plan of the Church
of St. Peter at Priko
near Omisa

(b) Plan and Section of Church of
S. Barbara, Trogir (Trau)

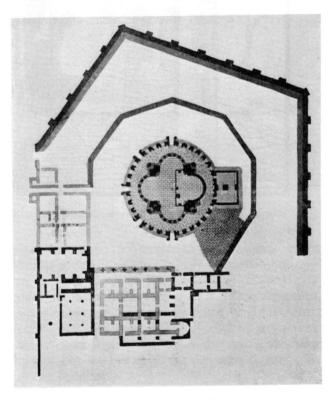

(c) Zwarthnotz, Armenia:
Plan of Cathedral and Patriarch's Palace

PLATE IV

(*a* and *b*) Rab (Arbe).   Altar Ciborium

(*c*) Kotor (Cattaro) Cathedral.   Altar Ciborium

In addition to these various domed types there are also long churches. I think the epithet "early Croatian" may be applied to those which contain one aisle only, and are barrel-vaulted. A considerable area is covered by these churches in the Dalmatian islands. Two types are found. The first has plain walls. I found the same type in Bohemia and Moravia, as I had also found it in Armenia, and it seems to me, considering the smallness of its dimensions to be an independent form. In Finland barrel-vaulted buildings of this kind are built by the peasants as potato-cellars. But there is another species of barrel-vaulted church in the Dalmatian islands which seems to me to be of great interest. In this the thin walls are buttressed inside and out by pilasters joined by blind arcades. This type is found particularly in

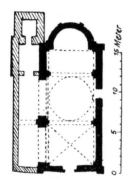
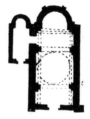

FIG. 15.—PLAN OF THE CHURCH OF S. MARIJA AT KOTOR (CATTARO).

FIG. 16.—PLAN OF THE CHURCH OF S. LUKE AT KOTOR (CATTARO)

the islands of Brač and Lastovo, and on the peninsula of Stona between Dubrovnik and Split. But the most highly developed examples are a number of churches in the region of Knin. Fig. 17 gives the plan of the church of S. George at Zestina. There we find a nave of 8·93 by 4·96 m., with an interior square apse measuring 1·14 by 3·30 m. outside. On both sides of the walls are blind arcades. The church is dated by an inscription with the name of Ljubomir Tepdzija whose earliest known date is 1088 ; but the type seems clearly much earlier.

The most instructive example of this class is S. Luka, 18 km. from Dernis, on the railway to Knin, near the village Uzdolje. I visited the ruin which lies in an interesting old cemetery on a hill. The only remaining portion is the lowest part of the walls (Fig. 18), the rectangle of 5·05 m. wide has at its east end a semi-circular apse and shows the blind arcades inside and out. Here the significant fact may be

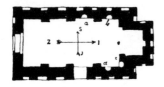

noted that the pillars on each side of the wall have no connection with each other. Some decorated fragments found in this small church and dating from the time of Mutimir (892-910) are on exhibition in the neighbouring Museum of Knin.

FIG. 17.—PLAN OF THE CHURCH OF S. GEORGE AT ZESTINA.

We are not in this chapter concerned (1) with the single-aisled churches with groined vaults, or (2) the interesting two-aisled type like S. Pietro at Zadar (Fig. 13), which is a good example, with its rectangular apses and squinches, and the church of Bublin, near Runović, with its rich ornament, or (3) with the three-aisle basilicas of a larger size found especially at Knin, such as the churches of Biskupija, Kapitul, and Stupovi. They are the connecting-links between the early Christian basilicas of Salona with wooden ceiling and roof and the great Romanesque vaulted basilical churches. So, too, the churches of Benedictine foundation, though of interest, form a group by themselves. None, however, of these forms seems to me to be typical of early Croatian build-ings, except for the great quantities found in them of orna-mental fragments, the remains of richly decorated stone furniture. In the plan of S. Luka, near Knin (Fig. 18), we see at the east end in the pilasters on the north and south two grooves. These mark the place of the screen dividing the sanctuary from the western portion occupied by the congregation. Similar indications of a screen are found in the so-called S. Martha church of Bihać, which, like S. Maria, near Salona, excavated by the Bihać society, is not yet fully published.

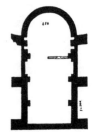

    B. *Ornament.*—All early Croatian decora-tion shows interlacing with bands of three striations. In the British Isles it appears as the first Teutonic element along with early Celtic and Roman designs : it is only later that the second stage is seen, the interlaced animal ornament. The finds in Dalmatia and

FIG. 18.—PLAN OF THE CHURCH OF S. LUKA, NEAR KNIN.

Croatia belong quite certainly to the former stage, with bands only. Animal ornament is used, but never with interlacing.

As I have said, this style of ornament is not often found on the buildings, but on the church furniture. Where ornament appears on the building, as, for example, on the door-lintels in S. Kriz at Nin or in S. Barbara at Trogir, it is certain to show some foreign element; it is not the pure interlaced band-motive. The field where this geometrical design finds greatest scope is the screen and the altar: it is seen also in some baptisteries, and other places. I select from the great mass of fragments some characteristic specimens in a good state of preservation.

The Screen.—Illustrated on Plate I. (*b*) is the screen of S. Martin's Church in the *Porta Aurea* at Split. There is an architrave on two columns stretching from wall to wall with a gable having a round arch cut in the lower part over the entrance. Two panels cover the lower portion. The triangular gable with arch is the main feature, which is definitely early Croatian. All the museums contain specimens, forming an extensive series, preserved mainly not only for the sake of the decoration but on account of the names of dukes and kings, etc. We, however, are concerned only with the decoration. I show later some more examples.

The Ciborium.—This also has the effect of a screen; it is not, however, joined to the walls, but comprises a rectangular slab on each side, with a semi-circular arch form cut out of each slab. These may be described as п-shaped from their resemblance to the Greek letter *pi*. They are frequently found in Dalmatia, but no well-preserved example is extant *in situ:* the only example which might be cited is in the Cathedral of Rab (Arbe), but there are only a few of the original pieces left, the whole having been reconstructed during the Renaissance (Plate IV. (*a, b*)). In the Museum at Zadar are preserved the four п-arches of the old domical ciborium, found in its campanile (Plate V. (*a*)). A less-known specimen shows (Plate IV. (*c*), after the drawing by Jackson) a п-arch of the altar-ciborium, now in the sacristy of the cathedral at Kotor, belonging to the first Tryphon-church of 809. The inscription gives the authenticated name of its founder.

A valuable monument of this kind was brought from Nin to Venice, namely, the baptismal font in the Correr Museum (now perhaps in the new Archæological Museum) with the name of Wičeslav (*c*. 800), one of the first Croatian dukes known by name (Plate VI. (*d*)). On each side is a pair of columns, and in the main field a cross in interlaced bands with the central rhomb, usual in Croatian art.   Possibly a good many of the " Vere da pozzo " of Venice may have been brought from the Croatian region of the Adriatic.

II. The Essential Characteristics of Ancient Croatian Art.—We noticed that the ancient Croatian churches are built for the most part on a very small scale, and that the ornament is designed by hand without any mathematical instrument. This gives us *a priori* a characteristic which is quite independent of the main period-divisions on the ground of style which are found in the usual histories of art.   Some years ago I tried to inculcate a habit of thought which should concentrate less on monumental size than on evidences of creative impulse, even when they appeared on a small scale and in a crude form.   We have now reached the stage of relegating the great monumental works rather more to the background.   We look beyond them to their sources.   We look beyond S. Sophia and S. Peter's and see that the cupola over a square bay buttressed by niches or barrel vaults was not the creation of Constantinople and Rome, but originated in the extreme east of Hither Asia.   The great cities and buildings have done no more than inspire ideas, the history of whose evolution, as we shall see in these chapters, is perhaps of greater interest for us than the standard monuments of architecture of the first rank.   It seems to me a fact of significance and value that the small rough buildings made by free hand on the Croatian coast and in the interior have, in the main, no connection with the great early Christian basilicas which preceded them before the immigration of the Yugo-Slavs, in Croatia itself and in Dalmatia.   That type is well known, and I need not describe it : the magnificent columns, and the pavement and wall-mosaic types frequently brought from other countries, are sufficiently familiar.   Here we are discussing only the early Croatian buildings proper.   The interest in those small and insignificant churches is confined to a few specialists.   But they are the nursery of early North European church art, of the round, the square, and the short slightly elongated churches with cupolas and barrel vaults near Prague, in Moravia, and in Spain.   If we arrange them in chronological order, the Visigothic group in Spain, of the seventh and eighth centuries, may be the earliest, then, in the ninth and tenth centuries, the Croatian, and, a little later, the West Slavonic group.   In the eleventh century, when Romanesque art grew up, these three early Northern European art-streams—one Teutonic and the other Slav—were still present. There is a second Teutonic stream which I omit, the Lombardic, in Italy, as it went its own way in architecture; the ornament on the church furniture, however, bears a strong resemblance to that of the Croatians.

Now what is the essential character of this early North European church art shown by the small Croatian stone churches on the Dalmatian coast and their decoration compared with the monuments in Spain, in Prague, and in Moravia?

It is these main groups of pre-Romanesque churches of which we must take account and study comparatively if we desire to pursue our researches more closely into the early art of Northern Europe as we have it preserved on stone monuments on the frontiers of the southern countries or actually in those countries. The southern peninsulas became the outposts of northern art. We can work backwards from them to the north, but we must not, as we have done hitherto, particularly with the art of Lombardy, assume that art necessarily expanded northwards from the south. To all appearances this art was first brought from the north to the south. It is those first monuments of the Dark Ages that concern us in these lectures, which connect both the streams of art of that period, the Franco-Lombard in Western, and the Byzantine in Eastern Europe. Later on I shall answer the question how West and South Slavs can be connected with so far distant a country as Spain. For the moment we shall only inquire whether the Christian art of Spain from the seventh to the eleventh century has any essential relation to the Slavonic art of Dalmatia, Prague, and Moravia.

The Spanish monuments are published in the *Monumentos Arquitectonicos*, 1859-78; Lamperez, *Historia de la arquitectura crist-Española;* Moreno, *Iglesias Mozarabes*, etc. The West Slavonic monuments are published by Lehner in the first volume of his *Dějeny umění naroda českého*, I., 1903.

1. *Raw Materials and Technique.*—Perhaps the only building of the early Croatian period on the east coast of the Adriatic, which is quoted in the comprehensive histories of art, is the church of S. Donatus in Zadar. It is built on a larger scale and may be called the standard example of early Croatian architecture. And this Rotunda, constantly compared with San Vitale at Ravenna or the Mausoleum of Charlemagne

at Aix-la-Chapelle, shows very clearly one of the essential characteristics of early Croatian architecture. Plate V. (*b*) shows some details of the foundations of this church; we see that it is made up of the remains of older buildings. As there was no tradition of stone architecture, the materials, often of the cheapest, were put together as they were found. The employment of the columns is astonishing and their foundation even grotesque, and it is a matter for wonder that they remained in their places and that the structure did not collapse.

This example attests the ignorance on the part of the early Croatians of what we should call cutting from the solid stone, especially freestone. They used field stones and quarry stones, binding them quite irregularly with mortar. I am laying stress on this crude stone technique, as it is of importance for all pre-Romanesque stone architecture. The North built for the most part in another raw material, namely wood, and in a later lecture we shall see what the architect in that medium could produce. Here I speak solely of stone. If we go to the Celts or the Teutonic and Slav peoples, we shall invariably find in their stone monuments the same rough workmanship. I was most forcibly struck by it in Finland. In parts of the Cathedral of Åbo and the church of Hattula a fine brick surface is seen, but this is exceptional. All the other " mediæval " churches of Finland are built of field stone, and are impressive by reason of their crude massive effect. There an impression may be formed of the appearance in the landscape of church architecture in the southern countries with a Teutonic or Slav population, some churches, in heavy masses of field stone, the rest in wood in blocks or in framework. In the present chapter we are considering stone exclusively.

A. *Architecture.*—The principal point to be observed about the early Croatian monuments is that they are not built like Roman or Romanesque buildings of regularly cut freestone, but of field stone and mortar, which, as I found, had been the only material known in Finland, and was also used, I think, in Gaul in addition to the *opus Romanum*, being the original *opus Gallicum*. In fact it is this unpretentious workmanship which gives to early stone architecture in Northern Europe its essential character. We are so much in the habit of considering only monuments exhibiting a finished technique in stonework, that we pay no attention to this significant stage. There is much interesting material in England and Ireland that would repay study in this connection.

The second fact about these rude buildings which is of more than ordinary interest, is that they are fully vaulted at a time when it is generally supposed that vaulting had not yet appeared in Christian architecture. It is not the familiar early Christian timber-roofed basilica, but this early North European art that must be considered in studying the evolution of the architecture of the middle ages. In Spain, too, as in Dalmatia and Armenia, we can see that light stones were employed in building the vaults; and in early Croatian ruins, as in the Visigothic monuments in Spain, we find tufa and porous stones, the remains of the once vaulted roof.

A third characteristic of all early Croatian buildings is their irregularity (Fig. 5). They are not the work of an architect with a previously prepared plan, but of artless masons. I was able to study this not only in Dalmatia and Spain, but nearer home in Finland.

While we base our opinions to-day on extant stone monuments, which from their nature are not so liable to destruction, we must not overlook the possible use of other materials which have perished with the lapse of time. We must take into account the possibility of monuments not having survived, and be on the look-out for traces of them. In considering the period at which North European art extended to the southern countries, our first question is whether some material other than stone or brick was predominant, such as wood. Thus we are led to ask whether there may not be two streams in pre-Romanesque architectural monuments, those which were originally conceived in stone, and others, which are merely wood architecture translated into stone in southern countries where wood was scarce. First of all, we may consider stone types. Pure stone types appear in all kinds of round building. Therefore, in spite of what we learn from literary sources, round buildings cannot be in the southern tradition: as I showed in my article in " Slavia," III., on West Slavonic art, we found them in indigenous types.[1] There I also demonstrated that stone churches copying wooden originals tended to be square: in the blockwork of Eastern Europe, as we shall see in the second chapter, the square form predominates with the barrel vault and cupola. In this chapter I shall merely summarize the explanations given hitherto of the fact

[1] For bastion architecture of this kind, cf. E. Brantiņš, *Latvijas pilskalni Zemgale un Augšzeme*, Riga, 1926.

that early Croatian churches are vaulted and built on the square plan.

B. *Ornament.*—From the great number of decorated stone fragments showing interlaced bands with triple striations, we already begin to surmise that this branch of early Croatian art cannot have been derived from any Mediterranean stream of art, as is commonly argued, but must bear some closer relation to the actual people employing this ornament for its church furniture. Is it too much to suggest that in the furniture of the household and of the royal palaces this motive is equally popular? Not unnaturally we cannot produce any objects of this kind, as they were almost certainly made in a medium which was unfortunately not likely to survive, namely, in wood. In the last chapter we shall be confronted with the very richly ornamented wood furniture of the far North, which will throw a vivid light on the unknown world of the Dark Ages. Is it conceivable that the art which delights us in Norway, preserved almost by a miracle, was not in existence also in the other Teutonic and in the Slav countries? We must remember, too, the extraordinarily rich ornament on the gravestones in the British Isles, and on the crosses, illuminated manuscripts and metal-work. It seems to me that the predilection for exuberant ornament on the part of all the northern nations is an undoubted fact: it is only in the East of Europe and in Armenia that the early buildings themselves show little or no ornament.

The interlaced three-striped bands of the early Croatian stone liturgical furniture are cut entirely by freehand, and are therefore of the same irregular character as the buildings themselves. If we look more closely, we shall find that it is precisely the three stripes that suggest woodwork : they are cut with the same bevelled surface (*nosch, scat, jag, Kerbschnitt*) as the best-known wood technique, with which we shall have to deal later.

2. *Significance.*—Are all the small buildings to be considered to be churches? It is certain that several of the round buildings with six niches inside were used as baptisteries ; others, with four niches, like S. Kriz in Nin, may have been used not only as churches, but as mausoleums as well. As I have already said in my work on Armenia, pagan buildings designed for quite a different purpose, and of a different material, could be utilized when men, having been baptized into the Christian faith, began to build churches. So it is with

the liturgical furniture. Among the many thousand fragments of early Croatian stone furniture we found no single
piece that would not probably belong to a church. What
does this signify ? If space permitted, I should show that
all these stone screens with gabled lintels are technically
built in framework, which is not typical of stone, but of
woodwork. And what of the ornament ? The interlaced
bands themselves have, at the present time, hardly any
other significance than mere decoration. We shall see that
they consist of circles, lozenges, and other geometrical designs,
and that the striations on the bands technically recall woodwork. But besides these ornaments there are symbols of
various kinds : crosses, niches, birds (peacocks and doves),
the pentagram ; these are certainly not early Croatian, but
Christian in origin, although a closer examination may reveal
traces of early Slavonic or Iranian influence.

3. *Shape.*—Students of the Visigothic monuments in
Spain, the Lombardic of Italy, the West and East Slavonic,
the Finnish and Armenian, will find shapes curiously akin to
these in the Croatian countries both as regards the architecture
and in the ornament. At the same time, however, there are
certain differences, which appear only on a closer inspection
and comparison.

Architecture.—While the material used for the Croatian
churches is field stone with mortar, the architectural forms
approximate to those of the commonly known stone buildings.
We may examine a few•individual types. The round type
which we found to occur frequently in the neighbourhood of
Prague and in Moravia, beginning at the end of the ninth
century, seems to be identical with the stone type of the
North European churches. This form may have owed its
origin to the necessity of defending the church, the round
shape being possibly derived from a bastion. Note the
arrangement of the windows in the church of S. Gospa
(Fig. 19), on the island of Vis (Lissa) : two small rectangular
windows on both sides of the door, with two circular windows
on the wall above. If, as is possible, this building dates from
a later period, it bears some resemblance to the mausoleum
of Theodoric at Ravenna. The round type with interior
pillars supporting the dome is very general in the island of
Bornholm in Sweden, and appears also sometimes in Germany
(Fig. 20). These fortified stone churches show marked
affinities with S. Donato at Zadar, having the same inner

circle of columns surrounded by the cupola, and the gallery. The most interesting example of this was a church in Schleswig (Fig. 21), which had the inner wall pierced by arches, and also the three round apses.   It is possible that this church is related in some way to an ancient Slavonic monument, in which case we could readily understand the same Slav type appearing in S. Donato at Zadar.

The square type, unusual in Roman or Romanesque times, is the typical shape for the intermediate period between these familiar styles.   In my opinion, the type-series of Lehner, whose knowledge of the churches in Bohemia and Moravia (Fig. 22) which I call pre-Romanesque or North European is

unrivalled, is correct, although his four square types rather incline to the rectangular.   But this is the prevailing tendency, as may be seen in Armenia, since the Syrian church, like the Byzantine and Roman churches from the beginning, gravitated towards the long rectangular shape, thereby influencing all countries in which the churches, rather than the Christian faith, were all-powerful, in the direction of the long church or,

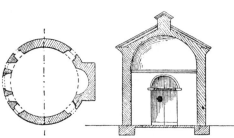

FIG. 19.—PLAN, SECTION, AND ELEVATION, CHURCH OF
S. GOSPA, VIS (LISSA).

at least, a species of compromise between the square and the long types.   In Croatian countries the square bay was, as we find, bounded in ancient Croatian times not by walls, as in the West Slavonic regions, but in the centre of the area formed by the combination of the square with adjoining enclosures, these last alone having walls.   Such combinations are the types usually known as the Greek cross church, the three and four-apse type, and that in which the cupola is supported by four pillars or columns, and buttressed by four barrel vaults over the aisles.   The cupola hall is one-aisled, and has also the cupola on pilasters between barrel vaults.   It is very often found in Serbia and Rumania.

Finally, the square or half-square is to be found in all

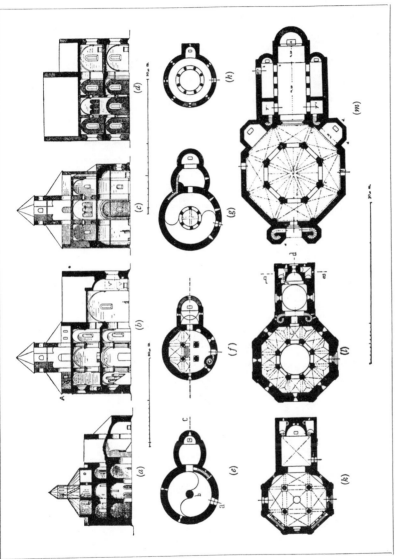

FIG. 20.—PLANS AND SECTIONS OF VARIOUS CHURCHES AT BORNHOLM (SWEDEN) AND IN GERMANY.
(a) Osterlars (Bornholm); (b) Heiligegeistk, Wisby (Gotland); (c) S. Ulrich, Goslar; (d) Ledöie (Seeland);
(e) Nylarsker (Bornholm); (f) Bjernede (Seeland); (g) Osterlarsker (Bornholm); (h) S. Michael, Fulda;
(k) Wisby (Gotland); (l) Storehedinge (Seeland); (m) Georgenberger Kirche, Goslar.

interiors where the transition to cupola or apse is effected by

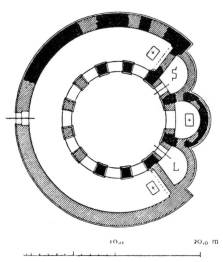

a squinch over the corner. A good many of these types may be found in Spain and Armenia also, but they are not typical of the art of the Lombardic period in Italy, where they do not appear until the eleventh century. With the square is associated a peculiar type of cupola. In the Croatian monuments of Dalmatia it has invariably a high conical shape inside, and is mostly without windows, having the shape of a tower. The transition from the square to the round is accom-

FIG. 21.—PLAN OF A CHURCH IN SCHLESWIG, GERMANY, NOW DESTROYED.

plished by means of squinches. These special shapes are

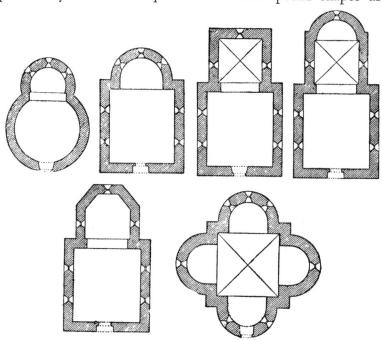

FIG. 22.—CHURCH TYPES IN BOHEMIA AND MORAVIA.

PLATE V

(a) Arch of stone altar-ciborium, Zadar (Zadar Museum)

(b) Zadar   substructure to Church of S. Donato, now a Museum

PLATE VI

(a) Zagreb. The Branimir Stone

(c) Typical Croatian surface ornament in stone (Drzislav)

(b) Stone Ornament from Cracovia (Wawel)

(d) Baptismal Font of Wiceslav now in the Venice Archæological Museum

found also in other places, being especially frequent in Spain and Armenia.   We shall see later the explanation of this feature.

The long type with barrel vaults over walls buttressed inside and outside by blind arcades is also to be found in Spain and Armenia.   The comparison of the Croatian blind arcades with the " Lisenen " of the early Christian churches of Ravenna is merely the old humanist tendency to rest content with tracing everything back to Italy and Rome.   With Croatian and Lombardic architecture such a comparison cannot be made, since in Italy the early Christian basilica was still prevalent in the Dark Ages, while in Dalmatia the appearance of wholly new types, having particular features of high importance, forces into the background what remained of the early Christian tradition in that country.

The blind-arcade ornament is as typical for Croatian monuments as for those of Spain and Armenia.   I shall deal with the question of its origin in the second chapter.   A very general feature in the churches in Spain and Armenia is the horse-shoe arch, which, however, is not typical in Dalmatia.

Ornament.—If we compare the Branimir stone (888) (Plate VI. (*a*)) with a relic.of the year 777, the chalice of the Duke Tassilo at Kremsmünster, a piece of rich metal-work, like the well-known English and Irish relics of the same kind, we shall notice an astonishing fact : the more northern Teutonic chalice shows, a hundred years before the stone, interlaced animals, a different, and, as we think, a later ornament, while the Croatian stone is decorated only by interlaced bands.   In the North, in the eighth century, an animal ornament ; in the South, in the ninth century, a pure geometrical design.   What is the explanation ?

Let us first consider the various geometrical shapes themselves.   One is inclined to suppose that the designs had their origin in textiles or in metal-work, or that they were invented by the Lombardic stone-workers, and so on.   We are justified in saying, in the first place, that in the North since Neolithic times these geometrical patterns have been found to be derived from the ornament on decorative handicraft ; and, secondly, that in the first thousand years of our era we cannot point to this or that material or technique as taking the lead.   At that time northern, by which I mean ornamental, art is highly developed, especially, as we shall see in later chapters, in wood. We find stripe patterns and similar designs indefinitely extended to fill out square or other surfaces. The patterns themselves are almost invariably circles, semi-circles, squares, rhombs, zig-zags in various combinations crossing, or interlaced with small circles. But there exist also a few examples of a free composition with animal combinations like the capital of Rab (Arbe) (Plate VII. (*b*)).

One of the most interesting patterns is the crocket, which we have noticed appearing on the sides of the gable (Plate I. (*b*)). It is identical (Plate VII. (*a*)) with that which we find later in Gothic architecture, where it is cut free. It must have been in existence before the Dark Ages as a free terminal motive in northern art : for the moment the place of origin and the material are an unsolved riddle. It is more germane to Croatian art than to Lombardic. Together with the gable, it is the rule in Dalmatia, while in Italy it is the exception. The scroll, where it appears, is not represented naturalistically, but is purely conventional.

4. *Form.*—While the shape is in all its manifestations geometrical, the form has a rhythm which is expressed by the round and square in architecture as in ornament, in spite of the fact that as late as the Dark Ages each is independent of the other. In architecture the round and the square may be considered separate and independent, but in combination they make up a formal unity ; in the ornament, on the contrary, each singly or both together may be combined with the rhomb in a lattice-pattern with no relation to a formal plan.

Architecture.—This remarkable predilection for the round and the square gives to the exterior block and to the space inside an appearance of massive unity, which lends a monumental aspect to the whole, even where the building is small in size. I had previously noted this as an artistic value in Armenia ; there, as in Croatia, Dalmatia, and Visigothic Spain, it is accentuated in the churches by the fact that architecture is not enhanced by ornament, the decoration consisting only of blind arcades which repeat to a certain extent the round and square combination. The proportions in these combinations count for much, but for the moment we cannot enter into details, as we require exact measurements for the monuments of various countries. It is a remarkable fact that in Spain and Dalmatia the small cupolas have no windows. In this respect Armenia shows independence, introducing into architecture the " tambour," or drum, a cylindrical structure with windows between the square and the cupola.

About the use of colour in architecture we can say nothing, but if we draw inferences from the variety of colours on the church furniture, the appearance of the inside of the churches must in some way have matched it. In the church of S. Trojstvo, near Split, I found in some of the six apses relics of stone balls in the zenith, which recalled the coloured water-bottles in the ornament of Cividale and in Spain.

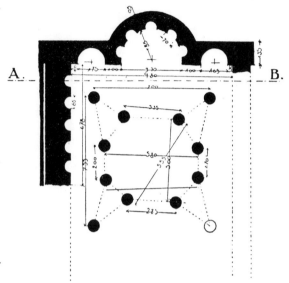

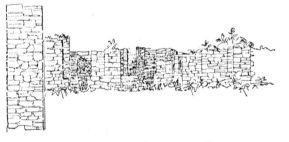

FIG. 23.—EXCAVATED BUILDING AT GRADINA, NEAR SOLIN.

A building of great interest which might well be thought to be the work of an early Croatian architect in a new formal style has been excavated at Gradina, near Solin (Fig. 23). There are twelve columns, three at each corner, with rectangular walls, and detail which is of great importance. Analogous to this is the Cathedral of Zwarthnotz (Plate III. (c)), the best known of the Armenian church types, in which the four main piers are of a massive L-shape, with a detached column in the angle, making the whole form roughly rectangular, as at Gradina. We shall bear this singular resemblance in mind, and in later chapters inquire whether there must not be some relation during the second half of the first thousand years after Christ between the art of Dalmatia and that of Armenia. Perhaps we shall find other explanations of this striking affinity.

Ornament.—This lies on the surface like network, the bands being raised on the ground ; the frame cuts the pattern at the end or in the middle of one of the units of ornament. The design is not always immediately obvious ; on the contrary, one has often the feeling of indefiniteness of design on the part of the stonemason (Plate VI. (c)). The ornament is evenly spaced on the surface ; there are no blank areas in the pattern. The only striking feature is the three striations on each band : the effect of light and shade given by oblique cut stripes contrasts effectively with the sunk surface round the bands. The museum of Zadar possesses several fragments with colours, the most favoured being blue and red with gold. Their date is not certain.

Originally the patterns all tended to run along in bands : a surface was filled by several parallel bands ; to fill out square surfaces with a continuous design which could be indefinitely extended was a new form.

5. *Content.*—In the first part of this chapter I should have liked to complete our knowledge of the monuments by the quotation of a list of names from inscriptions and ancient literature : those, for example, of the architects and sculptors. But it is no mere chance that we are ignorant of these names ; that seems to me to be an essential feature of the early Croatian art : the monuments are anonymous, the work of craftsmen who did not belong to the upper classes of society, but were men of the people.

The artist may be found also among the simple craftsmen. It may be that the name of " artist " was originally used only in the South, where a person commissioning a work of art was chiefly anxious to be portrayed himself, a fashion not known in the North before the invasion by southern culture. In the North there was no representational art, and therefore no critic to appraise the artist, for the purpose of history, at his true value. There is a further point. Documentary evidence of the early Croatian period, inscriptions and other sources, is all in Latin or Greek, and only one name occurs which might be that of an artist, Sumpertus, quoted in an inscription of S. Marta, in Bihać. Some scholars consider this to be proof that the Lombards were the creators of Croatian art ; others, however, point out that Sumpertus, like S. Marta and S. Martin, may have his origin in a Frankish country such as Provence.

On the whole, I do not think that Latin or Greek sources often contain the name of an indigenous architect or sculptor.

PLATE VII

(b) Carved Capital from Rab (Arbe)

(a) Carved Stone Gable with crockets, Knin

PLATE VII

(b and c) Bronze Bowl at Stockholm (Scandinavian Ornament of the Bronze Age)

(a) The " Prince " Relief from the Baptistery at Split (Spalato)

Lombardic Latin inscriptions give the Latin name Ursus as being that of a sculptor : in Spain alone, the Visigothic name of Tioda has survived as one of the architects concerned in the building of a monument.   My experience convinces me that the churches in Spain, Dalmatia, and Armenia, which belong to the early North European group are not in their essence Roman or Greek, Italian, or Byzantine, but the work of men of northern blood.   I was able to show the influence in Armenia of a master like Trdat on the evolution of Byzantine art.   In Europe the movement which began with the Romanesque period made it exceedingly difficult for a master in the early North European traditions to exert any influence. Only in course of time, and especially in the later " Gothic " architecture, did the enduring art of the early North European style become the deciding factor (see my new work, *Der Norden in der bildenden Kunst Westeuropas*).

Ornament.—The form used in early Croatian work is that of raised bands on the surface with a network of lines to fill out a given field.   These lines are expressive, and do not tire the eye like the North Germanic animal ornament, which we shall meet with in the fourth and fifth chapters.   This restfulness is found, too, in the Visigothic ornaments in Spain, the Lombardic in Italy, and the ornament of the far distant Armenia.   I illustrate here (Plate VIII. (*b*), (*c*)) one of the best specimens of Scandinavian ornament from the much earlier Bronze Age.   We see that there, too, the striped band is used, but without the interlaced network motive.   It is full of movement, like the later animal ornaments of these countries.

Now what is the explanation of the fact that not only the Armenian and Croatian band ornament, but also the Lombardic and Gothic, often have the characteristic restfulness ? Is it the influence of the Eastern European temperament ? Goths and Lombards were in contact with the East before they invaded Italy, Gaul, and Spain.   But the time has not yet come for an answer to these questions.

III. The Evolutionary Significance.—We have established two facts which throw a strong light on the Dark Ages as far as European art is concerned.   The Croats have, like the Western Goths in Spain, a vaulted architecture ; and, secondly, they use, like the Lombards in Italy, an interlaced band ornament for the stone liturgical furniture.   From these two facts alone we see at once the importance of the group of monuments with which we are now dealing.

We must remember that the Croatian churches belong to the pre-Romanesque period of European art, and that all humanists who have specialized in that period continually assert as certain and demonstrable facts that—

(1) There existed no vaulted church type in general use before about 1050.

(2) Interlaced band ornament is of Mediterranean origin, and spread from that source, especially from Byzantium and Lombardy, to the neighbouring countries of Europe.

Probably this chapter alone has shown that, if we consider carefully the monuments of what I call the early North European or pre-Romanesque period, we have vaulted architecture from the beginning. The basilica is the type which, as I have shown in my work on Armenia, hinders this evolution in some parts of Europe and in Asia. In Croatia we have seen the vaulted type to greater advantage than is possible in Italy, on which the humanists, in obedience to their traditional habit, have fixed their attention. There, indeed, the prevalent church type is, even in the Lombardic period, the early Christian basilica with timber roof and without vaults. That, however, is the exception. Beginning with Spain, and going as far as Armenia, the predominant type is a small vaulted church with a variety of round and square shapes.

As for ornament, we shall study in later chapters the northern art of Europe in the Scandinavian monuments before and shortly after the year 1000, that is to say, of a time when the influences from Greek, Roman, and Christian art had not yet destroyed the old indigenous tradition of northern art in Asia and Europe. At that time the connection of Northern Europe with the north of Asia, Iran, and India was apparently closer than with the South of Europe (cf. my article on the " Temple du Feu," *Revue des Arts Asiatiques*, 1927).

In the last centuries before the year 1000 the northern Asiatic stream of art with its animal decoration had given rise to the new Teutonic animal ornament of the migration period. Before the beginning of this movement in art, some of the northern peoples of Europe had migrated towards the South. The art-historians are, even in the matter of ornament, obsessed with the art of the Lombards in Italy. This people must have moved from the North earlier than the Anglo-Saxons, since they did not take with them the new animal ornament, but the earlier interlaced bands, which were especially familiar to the Iranians and Slavs.

It is strange that the Lombards preserved only this early ornament in the decoration of all church furniture in stone, altars, baptisteries, ciboria, pulpits, etc. No special attention has been paid to the group of ancient Croatian monuments on the east coast of the Adriatic. It is easy to group them along with the Lombardic monuments, and to say that they are only part of the Italian stream. As long as the conviction prevailed that the interlaced band ornament came from Byzantium, it seemed altogether natural that Dalmatia, being on the way from Byzantium to Italy, should be a part of this movement.

To-day, as I said first in 1891, we are agreed that the art of the Lombardic period in Italy is not a Mediterranean or Byzantine art, but belonged to the Lombards themselves; and there only remains the question whether they invented this style (Stückelberg) or, as I think, brought it from their north-eastern home or from their sojourn north and south of the Carpathians. I am much interested to see how scholars who consider the Lombards a creative people, explain the influence of their creation upon the whole of Northern Europe and Hither Asia. The development cannot be so explained. If we consider carefully the monuments of Dalmatia, we readily see that there is sometimes a distinct difference between these and the monuments of Italy. It may be possible to understand this difference which is absolute in architecture and relative in ornament, if we bring to bear evolutionary methods of research on the Europe of the Dark Ages.

1. *Persistence of the North.*—The remarkable fact that the early Croatian buildings show no regular stone cutting, no ashlar, speaks for itself. Further, it is significant that they are of small size and irregular construction, and, therefore, neglected in the general history of art. On this point we may make two observations. Scientists have found that the universe is affected not less by small phenomena than by the great astronomical forces : we may recall in this connection the amplitude of the problems connected with the movement of atoms. So the history of art must begin to take account of small things : these early Croatian churches, small in size and unpleasing in appearance, have values for the expert investigator comparable with those of the larger monuments called,

by the humanist, classical, or placed by him in some other broad category. The Croatian monuments, which are typical examples of the small things suggested above, have hitherto been supposed to possess a purely local interest.

Closely allied to this is another suggestion. There are two branches of science which prepare the way for this conception of the principles of art-history, both lacking what we call a philological and historical basis—pre-history and ethnology. They are closer to anthropology than to history, and are studied from the point of view of evolution rather than chronology. I wrote in 1923 a book, *Die Krisis der Geisteswissenschaften*, showing that we must begin to think rather of evolution than chronology in our history of art. Now the Yugo-Slavian or Croatian, like the early North European monuments, are precisely on the boundary-line between history and pre-history, between primitive man and the " higher culture." They have, therefore, been neglected by both sides.

In the last section (II.) on the essential character of early Croatian art, I employed the method of artistic comparison. Now let us see what influences arising from the geographical situation, the raw materials, the racial features, could make for permanence in the art of the Croatians between the Danube and the long coast of the Adriatic.

Architecture.—There are two features showing a measure of persistence to be found in the Croatian monuments, both to be observed in the only raw material preserved, but differing in technique. In contrast to the early Christian basilica, the small Croatian churches are vaulted, like those of Spain, Prague, and Moravia, but there is a difference between the round type and the square or rectangular. The one, I think, persists in stone. What of the other? There, too, I am sure a tradition persists. It is the intention of these chapters to show step by step how I myself formed this impression. But, first of all, we must complete our consideration of the theories now current, and in the next chapter I shall try to introduce to you the evidence which in time led me into an unknown world, and the art which by reason of its essential character and its evolution called for a fresh interpretation.

The only explanation of the affinities between the Visigothic monuments of Spain, the Croatian buildings in Dalmatia, and the Western Slavonic and Armenian churches is— as far as it appears in this or that analogy—that there must have been a movement from east to west : we shall come to that presently. At this point, however, we shall consider whether the enduring influence, not of movement, but of the geographical situation, raw material, and race is still of primary importance.

This question gives the connecting link to these chapters. The answer is to be found in the book itself. Dalmatia, more than the other Croatian provinces, is a southern country, part of the ancient Illyricum. Perhaps the influences making for persistence are to be found in the Illyrian tradition. But were the Croatians the first northern peoples to enter the Balkans ? Are not the Greeks, the Thracians, the Illyrians themselves northern peoples ? It seems to me that in architecture and ornament northern artistic values were already predominant in Greek art long before the final invasion of the Croatians, that is to say, in very ancient times. Later the same thing happened in the eastern movement from the Iranian east, and, indeed, the pure northern invasion of the migration period.

What we see in the early Croatian period cannot surely be the result of late Roman influence or the tradition of early Christian church architecture, both highly developed in the well-known monuments at Spalato and Salona. One can point to this or that feature as proof of such a tradition, but, on the whole, the early Croatian buildings, such as those in Spain, Prague, and as far distant as Armenia, show a different spirit, and the connection with those other countries indicates a persistence of raw material and technique in all the essential values of which we have spoken. Are we to assume an Armenian influence ?

Ornament.—If there is an Armenian movement in architecture, why has no suggestion been made of a corresponding movement in decoration ? In this matter experts are agreed in their conviction that interlaced band ornament is of Mediterranean, Byzantine, Lombardic, or Illyrian, generally Mediterranean, origin ; but fragments at least of this furniture with interlaced bands have been found not only in Dalmatia, but in Croatia itself, and in Slavonia as far as the bend of the Danube north of Belgrade, over which the Slavs once moved from the Carpathian countries of Transylvania to the Adriatic sea coast. Is it logical to ignore this fact ? We shall, moreover, see other remains of the same kind in the North proper. Must we not face the possibility that the Slavs possessed buildings and a decorative scheme, the type of which they brought across the Danube and established in all countries to which they emigrated. Is the migration of the ornament a satisfactory explanation? May there not have been in the East and North a creative centre, on which depended not only the art of Armenia but the art of the Goths, southern and western Slavs? Plate VI. (*b*) shows a unique stone panel with an interlaced ornament of bands with two strands, found in the Wawel of Cracovia. It is not difficult to distinguish the five rows of dependent triangles which are interlaced in lines suggestive of movement. It is another type, but akin to the Croatian and Armenian motives. The band of two stripes belongs rather to the Armenian, Iranian, and Byzantine character. May we not have here the centre for which we are inquiring, which must have been in the North, and of which we have other—later, I think—proofs from Jurjev-polskij, in the Vladimir district, north-east of Moscow. It seems possible that the three-stripe band rather characterises the northern, and the two-stripe the eastern provenance. As an instance, see the decoration of later Serbian churches such as that at Kalenic.

2. *The Demands of the Croatian Dukes and Kings.*—It is a striking fact that we found in the inscriptions in the churches and on the church furniture frequent allusions to a duke or king explicitly described as Croatian, and styled the founder. Thus it was that I alluded in the title of the chapter to Croatians. Now it might very well be the case that these dukes or kings, desiring works of art at their courts, borrowed artists from Byzantium or from the Lombardic or Frankish kingdoms, or even from the Pope of Rome; or purchased their first works of art in these places, thus introducing artistic influence from abroad.

Indeed, the local historians of art followed this line of interpretation. Mediterranean influence, aided by the desire of the Croatian potentates to imitate the Byzantine emperors and the Lombardic and Frankish kings, is put forward by the art-historians as an explanation of the Croatian art of Dalmatia. A visit to the museum at Knin ought to convince these experts of their error. The theory of a popular art derived from the artistic excursions of a despot is untenable. It is true that the will of the ruler was responsible for the introduction into Croatian art of the human figure. I show (Plate VIII. (*a*)) one of the rare examples of these exceptional works: it is merely a fragment.   A prince is represented in the manner familiar in Byzantine or Frankish royal representations.   But it is a copy by a designer of ornament.   A crowned and bearded figure is seated on a throne holding in his left hand a cross ; in the right, an orb.   On the left side a person in the attitude of *proskynesis*, with another figure standing over him.   The artist seems clearly unaccustomed to representing the human figure ; but shows an obvious zest in working the geometrical pattern over it.   The museum at Zadar possesses two interesting panels representing scenes of the youth of Our Lord (Plate IX.), the Byzantine type being followed ; but at the same time the ornamental features are present without any doubt.

3. *Southern or Eastern Movement.*—The first scholars to deal with the Croatian monuments were Eitelberger and Jackson, who wrote books on Dalmatia without, however, paying much attention to the pre-Romanesque remains.   It was the Italian scholars, for example, Cattaneo and Rivoira, who, while dealing with the monuments of that period in Italy, went on to consider the monuments on the other side of the Adriatic, treating them as Italian or, rather, southern.   Cattaneo took the interlaced band ornament for a Byzantine motive, while Rivoira saw in everything the universal creator, *Roma æterna*.

Those theories, which take no account of the persistence of northern art, turned in a new direction at the time when my volumes on the architecture of Armenia and Europe appeared, and after about five years came into the hands of the local authorities on the subject.   Bulić, the well-known archæologist of Split and Salona, following my lead, found that certain types of the early Croatian art have remarkable affinities with churches of about the same date, or earlier, in Armenia.   The same thing may be noted in the Visigothic monuments of Spain and the earliest West Slavonic monuments of Prague, Cracovia, Moravia, etc.   Let me point out some of the similarities.

In the first place, the pre-Romanesque or early North European monuments are vaulted, as the Armenian churches certainly were from the seventh century.   The plans are the same, barrel vaults and cupolas over a square plan and, in particular, the transition from the square of the walls to the circle of the cupola, effected, as in Dalmatia, by means of the squinch.   I might demonstrate that it is precisely the squinch that is the constant feature inside and outside the buildings in

Armenia, so that it seems to symbolize the origin of Armenian art. We shall have to deal with it in the second chapter.

The second main point of similarity between the pre-Romanesque monuments of the Goths, the Croatians, and the Western Slavs, is that those types, built on the square plan, and therefore, unlike the round churches, not invariably of stone, are also to be found in Armenia. Now let us inquire more particularly whether it is possible to assent to the theories expounded in my work in two volumes, *Die Baukunst der Armeniern und Europa*, 1918. If so, we should agree that vaulted architecture, especially that based on the cupola joined to the square plan by means of squinches, and at the same time interlaced band ornament, are in the Mediterranean countries the result of an Iranian and later Armenian movement. Might this be a solution of the problem? With this thought in our minds we may enter upon the next chapter.

PLATE IX

Zadar Museum.   Panels carved with scenes in the Life of Our Lord.

PLATE X

(a) Velike Mlaka (Croatia).   Chapel of St. Barbara

(b)   Detail of Wooden Roof in the Church at Sedlarica (Croatia)

CHAPTER II.

WOODEN ARCHITECTURE IN EASTERN EUROPE.

In the first chapter we found that the small early Croatian churches had no connection with the basilican churches of the same period in Italy and the Mediterranean, but were related to those of the western Goths in Spain, both having affinities with the distant Armenian churches. I could cite several authorities who consider all of these various kindred streams of art belonging to the first thousand years of our era to be dependent on Armenia. There is just a possibility that the Goths may have been the transmitters, who for centuries lived on the borders of the Black Sea, and, as I have shown in my work on Armenia, certainly had direct relations with Armenia itself, and had passed in their migrations through Asia Minor. At the end of the previous chapter I suggested that there might be an explanation of these affinities.

Now what is the nature of these affinities? As I have shown in my book, *Die Krisis der Geisteswissenschaften*, 1923, we must distinguish in practical research, as opposed to theorizing, three different affinities. In the first place, we have the most superficial of all, analogies between one monument and another. If we can show further that two monuments are akin, not only in appearance but in their essential character and artistic values, we have the second and more important affinity. True affinity exists, from which logical deductions can be made with certainty, provided that the essential kinship can be proved to rest on uniform processes of evolution. Of which kind is the affinity of the pre-Romanesque monuments of Europe and Armenia? Our deductions in the first chapter showed us that this affinity is not a mere superficial likeness, but that there are certain essential features suggesting more than a chance resemblance. But how are we to explain such a relation? If the Goths were the transmitters, it makes intelligible to my mind the connection of Armenia not only with Spain, but also with the Croatians. There is a theory—it is no more than a suggestion—that the Croatians were themselves Goths, just as the Bulgarians were originally Turks. But how are we to explain the appearance of these affinities in countries with which the Goths never had dealings, such as Bohemia, Poland, or Moravia ? In my work on Armenia I have already tried to discover a relationship between the most characteristic feature of Armenian and Iranian architecture, the cupola on squinches over the square, and the old Indo-Aryan wood architecture. Let me recapitulate here some of the steps in this problematical investigation.

I found that the squinch, a structure placed across the corner, built by the Iranian peasants of the present day in unburnt brick, and also found in ancient Persian palaces in concrete, stone, and burnt brick, has a certain relation to a similar corner structure in Kashmir, where, in small stone temples, we find an imitation of an earlier wooden roof with beams laid across the corner of a square forming a rhomb. A similar method of construction is followed to-day in wooden churches of the Ukraine, which show cupola-types in the same arrangement as at Périgueux, S. Mark's at Venice, the church of the Holy Apostles at Constantinople, or the church of S. John at Ephesus, three cupolas in a line, or five arranged in the form of a Greek cross. These dispositions are frequent in Iranian architecture of all periods. Can it be that they are a translation into stone of an older wooden prototype of the unburnt brick of Iran, finding its way thence to the Near East and Europe, especially in the form of the Armenian church on a square plan with the cupola on squinches ?

I propose in this chapter to pursue another train of thought, and to suggest that in the Dark Ages, from A.D. 600 to 1050, a material other than stone or brick may have been predominant, namely, wood, which was in its nature perishable, and that the monuments made in this medium have been lost ; as a consequence of which we are in a state of ignorance about the period. This theory has sometimes been put forward as a hypothesis, but never considered seriously. To begin with, as far as Western Europe is concerned, it is exceedingly difficult to publish the written evidence on early North European art, as it is not for the most part in Latin, but in one or other of the northern languages : in this way I could show that in Western Europe, in the Teutonic countries particularly, but also in the Celtic, wood architecture was general before the Roman Empire, and, later, before the Roman Church attained the height of its power. That must be the first step. Then we shall look for monuments.

I hope that my small institute at Vienna, having amassed the available information about all the extant wooden churches in the West, may be able to prove from the evidence of inscriptions, on the one hand, and on the other hand by deductions from the monuments of the later period that the West European building technique in wood was framework. We shall see in the fourth chapter that a different building technique in wood was employed in the north-western corner, in the region of the North Sea, and the explanation of this will be found in that chapter.

In Eastern Europe it is much easier to supply evidence of the important part played by wood, not only in the Dark Ages of European art-history, but also at the present day. There we have not only the extant written sources, but, above all, the monuments themselves to guide us. The number of wooden churches in Eastern Europe is so great that the task seems impossible, first of classifying them, and afterwards considering their essential character and explaining their evolution.

As far as we know, no mediæval wooden churches have survived in Eastern Europe. The preservation of the superb mediæval wooden churches in Norway, like the existence of the Alhambra in Spain, is a mystery. These we shall have to treat in the fourth chapter. The Slavonic world provides no such interesting mediæval puzzles. We must make up the deficiency for ourselves by deducing from the more recent monuments which still exist, the earlier monuments now lost. It is only by the employment of such a method that material can be gained for historical investigation.

In the first chapter we had constantly to distinguish between architecture and ornament. In the third and fourth chapters we shall see the rich ornament once prevalent in Northern Europe at the period to which belong the early Croatian churches. The present chapter is concerned with the east of Europe, where the churches are not richly decorated. We must not forget that the early Croatian stone churches may be said to be without ornament : only the church furniture shows the interlaced bands. It may be that the essential feature of eastern wood architecture is plain building, and that for the study of ornament we must, as in the early Croatian monuments, look for church furniture.

It is much to be regretted that the church furniture of the later periods is not the old popular peasant art ; as in the village churches of Western Europe, it is subject to the latest fashion. The church authorities themselves rejected the tradition of local handicraft, and, as I observed in Finland, gave the commission for the decoration and furniture of the church to a professed artist, for preference one whose education had been completed in Western Europe. Thus it is not surprising that we have nothing to say in this chapter on the subject of ornament. It has been destroyed along with the church furniture.

I. Study of the Monuments.—It is true that the archæology of wooden church building in Eastern Europe, like that of ordinary house building, is neglected by historians of art. It is not, however, unknown. The modern architect, having to construct villas or rural buildings of wood for less exalted purposes, is interested in the technique of ancient wooden architecture. Broadly speaking, we may say that, if woodwork is no longer held in high estimation, there is still a tacit appreciation of craftsmanship in wood, and we can see an admirable tradition preserved by the peasant population. It is a wide field which now lies open before us, about a thousand years after one of the most flourishing periods of this art in the North of Europe. Here, just as, for example, in the case of oriental carpets, we deduce the development and the richest period from the meagre remains.

We are concerned with church architecture only, and the number of extant monuments is great. I shall try as far as possible in this chapter to summarize the material, beginning with the question of the dates.

When I was writing my article, " The Beginning of the Pre-Romanesque Church Architecture of the Western Slavs " (*Slavia*, III., 1924), I came across a statement to the effect that the most ancient wooden churches extant were to be found in Silesia ; for instance, one of the tenth century in Smograu, and two others, 1204-1205, in Syrin and Lubom. The first of these does not appear to exist to-day, and the others are not earlier than the sixteenth century. The oldest examples that I myself know of are in Eastern Galicia : the earliest of these is published in my work on *Armenia*.

The technique of all these eastern churches may be described as blockwork [1] (logwork), that is to say full timber construction. I propose to give an account of the eastern

---

[1] I have made use of this term throughout to designate full timber construction as opposed to *framework* (half-timber), or *stave-work*. I am aware, however, that it is not a current expression in English architectural terminology.

block churches by describing important examples of each type, beginning with the extreme north and working southwards to Croatia. Investigations in Belgrade showed that there are no wooden churches in Serbia. It is, indeed, worthy of note that this fact forms to-day a boundary between Croatians and Serbians.

I shall be interested to see whether a more thorough examination of the question will confirm or refute what seems to me to be the fact, that in the purely Serbian area there is to-day no trace of the singular Croatian vaulted church types which are related, as we shall see, to wooden block architecture, nor any sign of the stereotyped interlaced band ornament dating from that early period, as in Croatia. These are curious and remarkable points, which I hope will help to arouse an interest in South Slavonic cultural problems.

We must also distinguish between the groups of eastern people, those of the Orthodox Church, on one side, and on the other the Catholic Slavs of the western frontier, and the far-distant Finland, which has been for centuries Protestant. I begin with the extreme North.

A. *Block Walls with Raftered Roofs:* (a) *Finland.*—We shall see later in Lapland a church (Sodankyle) with a beam roof proper. All the others known to me have roofs with rafters, an importation, I think, by the Catholic Church and the monks of the Germanic West. At the same time, almost all of the churches in Finland are vaulted. It was here that I first met with this curious combination of wood and vaulting. I had, with some diffidence, suggested such a combination in my work on Amida, expecting the idea to be greeted with universal derision. But I was obliged to follow where my material led me, and if I can establish my point, it may cause some slight disturbance to the slumbers of our placid humanistic art-historians.

In Finland, as in Croatia, there are two main types of churches—cruciform churches with an open square in the centre, and long churches. The main difference between stone and wooden churches in Finland is that while stone churches have normally three aisles, wooden churches have only one. I consider here only the wooden types.

One-aisled Churches with Block Pillars.—It will be understood that if the wall is made to bear both the roof and the vaulted ceiling, it will be in danger of falling. The larger the church the more the buttressing required. Now I found in Finland a highly interesting type of buttress, identical with the " Gothic " type, in wood, not stone, which I call block pillars. They are hollow, of short (1·20 mm.) beams, and set up so that the wall passes through them, and they are seen inside and outside having the appearance of wall pillars. Fig. 24 illustrates such a church (Saloinen, Salo), showing the long, aisled type and the pairs of block pillars ; they support

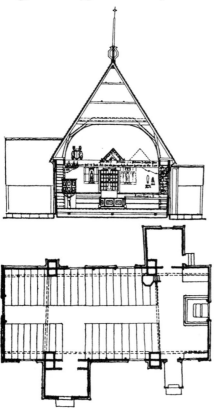

inside brackets in the direction west to east which take the beams for the barrel-vaulted ceiling, and in the direction north to south, the anchors to fix the walls ; outside, they support the single frames of the rafters ; in this roof under the rafters is a wooden ceiling consisting of boards secured by nails.

Cruciform Churches.— As a substitute for the block pillar we may find supports at the angles if there is a central square. Plate XI. (*a*) and (*b*), and Fig. 25 (Kiminki), gives some idea of this type. It might be said that there are two pairs of pillars, namely, those at the inside corners. It will be remembered that this type is familiar in Croatian,

FIG. 24.—PLAN AND SECTION OF THE CHURCH   South Germanic, and Ar-
AT SALOINEN (SALO).   menian stone churches.

Each of the four arms of the cross has its barrel vault ; over the central square there may be either a ceiling where these vaults cross, or a cupola proper.

(*b*) *Western Slavs.*—In my article on the " Pre-Romanesque Church Art of the West Slavs " (*Slavia*, III., 1924), I showed that the square, which in Finland is found only as the open square in the centre of the cruciform churches, was to be seen in its original form, with the four block walls (Fig. 22). It was only with the introduction of the roof with rafters, which in course of time was admitted in the Catholic frontier regions of Eastern Europe, that the square form gradually gave place to the rectangular and elongated types (Figs. 26 and 27). But while, as in Finland, the barrel-vaulted ceiling in the raftered roof was once typical, from the Renaissance onwards we find only the flat ceiling.

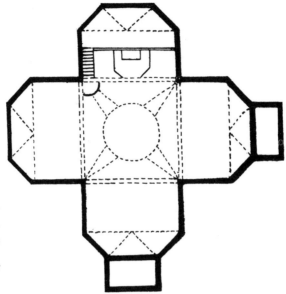

FIG. 25.—KIMINKI (FINLAND). PLAN OF CRUCIFORM CHURCH.

The work of Burgemeister on the wooden steeples and

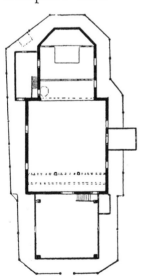

FIG. 26.—PLAN OF RECTANGULAR CHURCH AT KOMROWICE, NEAR BIALA (POLAND).

churches of the eastern provinces of Prussia gives good examples, the best being those from Silesia (cf. Strzygowski, *Die Holzkirchen in der Umgebung von Bielitz-Biala*, 1927).

(*c*) *South Slavs.*—Wooden churches, as I have said, are found only in Slavonia and Croatia, not in Dalmatia or Serbia. I hope that the present chapters may stimulate interest in these questions, and that in time material may be forthcoming from Bosnia and the Lika, a district north of Dalmatia on the Croatian coast, both rich in forests.

Plate X. (*a*) shows the chapel of S. Barbara at Velika Mlaka in Slavonia, near the Bosnian frontier, of late date (1822). By the kindness of the *Hrv. narodni muzej ethnografski odio u Zagrebu* I am allowed also to reproduce drawings of this (Fig. 28). We see a blockwork building with a raftered gable roof (Plate X. (*a*)). In the foreground is the wooden sacristy; in the background on the right, the steeple, on the west side of the long church. The nave is 9·40 m. (7·15 m.) long, 6·20 m. broad, and divided by two wall pillars. At the end is the apse, formed by three unequal sides of an

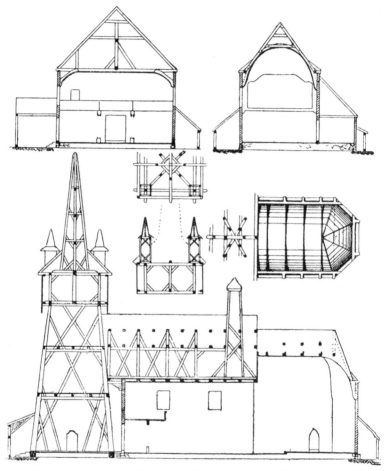

FIG. 27.—SECTIONS OF CHURCH AT KOMROWICE, NEAR BIALA (POLAND).

octagon. At the west end is a small gallery supported by two columns. If we look at the church in section we shall find that the nave is barrel-vaulted with boards attached with nails to the rafter structure.

Plate X. (*b*) shows a similar barrel vault from another Croatian church at Sedlarica, a Catholic church in Croatia itself, near the north-east frontier of the district of Bjelovar. This dates from the first half of the eighteenth century.   We have the Baroque altar, over which is the high wooden vault with the characteristic panel in the centre.   The surface is divided up by ribs into sections which are decorated with painted ornament, the work of a peasant.

B. *Pure Blockwork*.—I am not aware to what extent block-work is known in the Asiatic North, or what are its boundaries: it is probable that in the ancient Russian territory a prevailing type is to be found along with some of the features of Chinese wooden buildings.   Using ethnological maps, for example, that of Byhan in Buschan's *Illustrated Ethnology* (II., 1), North Asia, I find that the block-building region extends from South-east Russia to Iran, and that it is divided from China by a wide circle of tent-dwellings.   As I have said, I had to deal first with the Russian and Iranian material in my book on *Armenia*, and I was there concerned parti-cularly with the type of monuments in South Russia and in the eastern part of the former Austro-Hungarian Empire (cf. the first volume of the new journal *Armeniaca*, and Petranu, *Bisericile de lemn din judetul Arad*, 1927).

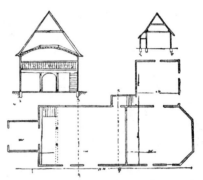

FIG.   28.—VELIKA MLAKA (SLAVONIA). LONGITUDINAL CHURCH :   PLAN AND SECTIONS.

To-day the division in the south-east corner of Europe round the Black Sea is no easier.   There the central region appears to be the Carpathians.   Such pure block churches as we find in Czecho-Slovakia, Poland, Rumania, and the Ukraine come from this crescent of forest.   We must not, however, forget that in Russia there was at one time another immense forest extending diagonally through Russia from the Baltic to the Kuban.   It is possible that this supplied material for the Slavonic block-building, and that the Carpathians were of secondary importance.   At present we cannot pronounce with certainty upon these points, as the art-history of the earlier periods does not ordinarily take the economic and geographical factors into account.   We can only say that the existence of the forests of Russia and the Carpathians may be assumed to have produced a wood architecture, which is only possible where forests are in abundance.

(a) *Barrel Vaults with Horizontal Beams*.—I can vouch for the possibility of this from my knowledge of Finland, and I shall show three illustrations of churches, one from Lapland, one in the Carpathians, the third in the Austrian Alps, which seem to be of a kindred construction.

In Finland, simple block-building of this kind is seen in the building of old houses. A drawing from Sirelius' book on primitive houses of the Finnish-Ugrian peoples illustrates the type (Fig. 29). We see that two of the four block walls end with a gable of shorter beams, and that from one gable

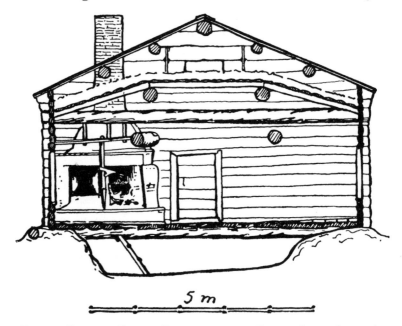

FIG. 29.—PRIMITIVE TYPE OF BLOCK-BUILDING IN FINLAND (AFTER SIRELIUS).

to the other extends not only the roof, but also the beams for the barrel-vaulted ceiling.

The church of Sodankyle, in Lapland, built in 1689, appears to be roofed in this way. On the west façade the beam-ends of the roof are visible in the gable, and it must be understood that the beams forming the barrel vault had to be laid in two parts, as the church was too long for a single beam. In the wall is the outside of a pillar, the inside of which would support the junction of the beams. As I was unable to examine this monument on the spot, I must leave it an open question.

PLATE XI

(c) Church at Apscha (Slovakia)

(a and b) Exterior and Interior of the Church at
Kiminki (Finland)

PLATE XII

(*a*) Church of the Trinity, near S. Veit (Carinthia)

(*b*) Detail of Interior of Roof of the above

Plate XII. (*a*) shows the little church of the Trinity near S. Veit in the Austrian Alps (Carinthia). The apse and

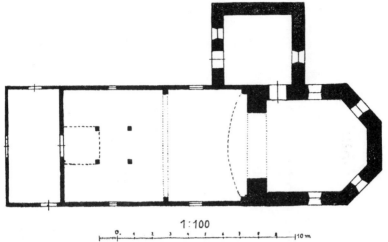

1:100

FIG. 30.—PLAN OF THE CHURCH OF THE TRINITY NEAR S. VEIT (CARINTHIA).

sacristy are built of stone, but the nave is of wood and dates from 1785 or later, while the western end with the belfry is 1865. Plate XII. (*b*) shows the interior of the roof, and the barrel vault of beams proper (13 by 15 cm.). They rest with their inner ends on an arch cut in wood, as shown in Fig. 31. The whole is secured to-day by an iron anchor. In front of the block wall is a pillar supporting arch and ceiling. The plan is given on Fig. 30.

A very interesting barrel-vaulted type is found in the Slovakian district of Szatmar. Experts may not believe in the existence of a true basilica without columns ; and, indeed, it is only conceiv-

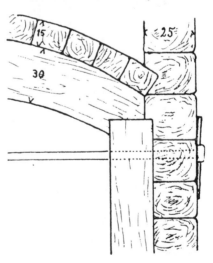

FIG. 31.—S. VEIT. DETAIL OF CONSTRUCTION.

able in very highly developed blockwork architecture. It may be asked if the column is not an essential part of what we call a basilica. The answer is surely that it is not, if the work of the column can be done otherwise. Fig. 32 illustrates

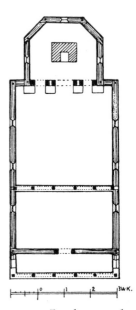

FIG. 32.—PLAN, ELEVATION, AND SECTION OF
THE CHURCH AT SZINEY-TAYALJA (SLOVAKIA).

this type. It shows the plan of a long church of the stereotyped pattern, in which, however, a screen encloses a square space in front of the presbytery; the deep apse is partitioned off, and there is an iconostasis with three doors. Now it is precisely this square nave that I call a basilica without columns. There is a high vaulted nave. The barrel vault lies not on the walls themselves, but on beams supported by consoles which reach to the point where, in the Roman basilica, the column stands.

There we have the beginning of a species of upper wall resting on exterior consoles, at its furthest end supporting the
barrel vault, which consists not of boards but of true beams.
We have a true vault, not merely a false vault in wood; over
it lie the rafters. Plate XI. (*c*) shows the exterior of such a
church.

(*b*) *Pyramidal Roofs* (*Cupola*).—If after the building of the
walls no gables or gabled roofs with barrel-vaulted ceiling are
added; if instead the square is to be roofed by a structure of
equal sides proceeding upwards and inwards from the walls,
the result is a roof of pyramidal shape. It may be constructed
in various ways. I shall not discuss this for the moment, but
shall first illustrate the various types from their exteriors.

North Russia.—The architecture of the northern portion
of the once great forests has been studied to some extent.
I discerned its influence on the Karelian frontier of Finland.
It is marked by a preference for the pyramidal roof over the
square plan : good examples are seen in the Russian provinces
of Archangelsk and Vologda. In Finland it is built with
rafters, in Russia by pure blockwork : the pyramidal roof has
its origin in this technique. I shall not dwell on the North
Russian monuments, our object being to consider whether
common old-Slavonic wood architecture had an influence on
the characteristic early Croatian types.

Ukraine.—A serious study of the South Russian wooden
churches has been made by Pavlucki in the first volume of his
Antiquities of the Ukraine, 1905. It was only with this book
at hand that I was able to write the chapter on this region in
my work on *Armenia*. There the typical plan for the building
of churches is on a square plan as a foundation : the church
is an aggregate of squares in one or two dispositions, three in
a line (Taraz, Plate XIII. (*a*)), or five crosswise (Chodorow,
Fig. 33). The roof again has a characteristic form : it is
built in the shape of a pyramid. This fundamental form is a
technical necessity where sloping beams are used for the roof.
We shall come to this point later.

This type can also be studied in the eastern provinces of
Czecho-Slovakia and Poland, on both sides of the Carpathians.
In Northern Galicia innumerable churches of this kind exist.
For several years I have been collecting all that I could find
in photographs and drawings, but it seldom happens that I
find a second representation of the same monument. I can
show only a few examples here. The most interesting building

is that seen in Plate XIV. (*a*) : in the foreground the steeple, in the background the church of Tarnawka as it appeared in April, 1915. The first impression one receives is of a Chinese temple. The roofs are arranged in steps : three, four, five, and more of the shingle roofs alternate with the gradually narrowing walls, the topmost pyramidal structure being crowned by a finial. The lowest roof serves as a buttress surrounding the walls. There are few windows.

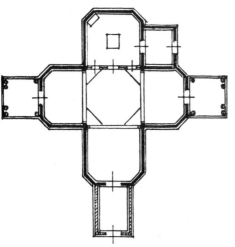

FIG. 33.—PLAN OF THE CHURCH AT CHODOROW (UKRAINE).

Plate XIII. (*b*) shows the church of Soko-lowka. The form is clearly different from that of the preceding example. On the central square is an octagonal structure below the bell-shaped cupola. At the corners are seen exterior triangles each roofed by part of a pyramid. The cupola on the west side is again a pyramid on walls built on a larger square plan. What sign is there of a transition here ? The cupola on the right is that of the apse, which forms three sides of an octagon, but the cupola is itself an octagonal structure. There are as many cupolas as varieties of construction. The whole building is surrounded by a modern cloistered walk ; but the walls and the cupolas show for the most part the old shingled surface, which in the original produces a high æsthetic effect with its wonderful succession of grey tones in light and shade.

II. The Essential Character of Wood Architecture with Horizontal Beams.—I hope to have given the impression that this type of building is governed by rigid unalterable laws which, taken together, indicate its essential character. But it is astonishing to contemplate the variety of types found in pure blockwork and in raftered buildings. There are, however, limits to the possibilities.

In this connection I may draw attention to the remarkable old houses in all parts of England. In London, Bristol, and

PLATE XIII

(a) Church at Taraz (Ukraine): South View

(b Church at Sokolowka (Northern Galicia

PLATE XIV

(a) Tarnawka (Northern Galicia).   Steeple and Church

(b) A Typical Block Pillar of the Finnish Type (Saloinen)

other towns, I saw wooden houses built in the Western European technique which I call framework. Certainly they are not on the same artistic plane as the great English cathedrals, each in itself a world in stone. But I confess that I am deeply moved by the sight of those old houses, which seem to me to contain the essence of the early English character. It seemed to me that there must be some churches existing in this technique ; we shall consider them in the third chapter. I mention these matters here only in order that I may be understood in the contention that I am about to make, namely, that the essential character of the old wooden churches in blockwork might be also identical with the Eastern feeling for home. These numerous monuments have given us a far greater insight into the life of the people than the great stone buildings of the East. One frequently finds there that if a stone building is of special interest, there is something in it derived from native wood architecture. The time may not be far off when we shall look out for such derivations and place more importance upon them than on the broad international styles.

We do not know how far east this block-building goes, but if I am right in my work on Armenia in tracing the origin of the square cupola on squinches to the Indo-Aryan migration, that is to say, from wood building of this type brought to the south to the Iranian unburnt brick building, then this architecture must be very ancient, and extends from the north to the mountains behind Iran and India.

Perhaps we may best conceive the situation if we envisage Armenia as having been at one time surrounded by countries with blockwork architecture. I found the pyramidal roof in Mylasa, on the coast of Asia Minor, and the well-known Lycian tombs show in part an imitation of blockwork in stone buildings, sometimes with the barrel-vaulted roof. But here we have to do only with Christian and pagan times just before the building of Christian stone churches. In my work on Armenia I did not sufficiently take account of the theory that in the early stages of Armenian church evolution the square blockwork with pyramidal barrel-vaulted roof was perhaps still in existence. Now we have material for comparative study, since we have to consider not only Iranian and Syrian brick and stone building, but also the northern woodwork (cf. the journal *Armeniaca*, I.).

That is one part of our research. The other is to keep in mind what we have learned from the Croatian monuments, which are some of the best examples of early North European or pre-Romanesque art in the East. Visigothic Spain, indeed, belongs to the West, but those Goths came from the Black Sea.

1. *Raw Materials and Technique.*—Wood is the only living raw material used in architecture. The consistency of the different kinds of wood is very various, according to the disposition and flexibility of the fibres. For example, there is clearly a great difference between the timber of the oak and that of the pine. The hard wood of the oak must be cut in quite a different manner from that of the softer wood of a pine or a fir tree. And if we remember that oak and other foliaceous trees come to an end on a certain northern frontier, we realize that there is a difference between the buildings of the more northern and the more southern parts of the northern area. The wood of the oak tree is cut in short heavy blocks ; that of the pine and fir in long beams. We shall see at once the result of this not only at the present time, but in all ages. It has a considerable influence on the shape and also on the form and content of a building.

It is certainly true that we also find in England peasants' dwellings built with horizontal beams. But it is to be noted that only the walls are built thus, not the roof. When he comes to the roof the builder changes his technique, using not horizontal beams, but rafters. We observe, therefore, in such houses a mixed technique, blockwork for the walls and framework for the roof. Now, to understand clearly the great difference between wooden churches in Western and Eastern Europe, we have merely to bear in mind that the characteristic technique of the West is framework, of the East blockwork. Where we find, as in Finland or in the Western Slavonic countries, rafters used for the rood-screen, we may be sure that western influence is present, as, for instance, in the Catholic church art of Finland.

The most important technical feature of all pure block-buildings is that they are vaulted. If we consider the process, this will seem quite natural. There are two possible means of roofing a block-building without departing from the system of horizontal beams, the one leading to the barrel vault, the other to the cupola. It depends upon the procedure adopted at the point where the roof begins.

The Barrel Vault.—The conviction that the barrel vault in wood is to be considered as imitating vaulted stone churches is a common one, although in some countries—Finland, for example—it is not easy to refer to barrel-vaulted stone churches.   It is greatly to be desired that we should begin to face these problems without blinkers.   We saw two kinds of barrel vault in block churches—the eastern with true beams, the western with nailed boards.   Let us once again study both processes.

By building with horizontal beams in the gable one kind of barrel vault is achieved.   One beam is laid over another on two sides of a square or rectangle, but each shorter than the other.   As they grow gradually shorter they form the gable.   For the roof itself long beams are required as for the walls.   So in the far North a technique of roofing is found in which these long beams are laid horizontally from gable to gable (*Pfettendach*).   In houses of this type, too, the barrel vault appears, in the construction of which long beams are used for the ceiling as for the roof, particularly necessary in the North on account of the cold winter.   Fig. 29 gives an illustration.   The beams lie symmetrically graded on the gable, and the ceiling consists of boards nailed on *bows*, or ceiling joists, fixed on the beams.   The barrel vault is therefore *boarded up*.   Fig. 31 and Plate XII. (*b*) show the other type with true beams.

For building with rafters the first method may be followed, that is to say, a vault consisting of framework with nailed boards, which is the technique generally employed in Finland (Fig. 24).

In the southern region of the northern area there is also the true barrel vault in wooden churches, a vault with beams cut wedgewise and placed together so as to form a vault of semi-circular form.   Are we to suppose that all these types are copied from stone prototypes ?   May it not be, on the contrary, that we should study one or the other process, so that we may come a little nearer to the origin of the barrel vault in wood or brick architecture.   When I was writing my work on Armenia, I had not made the discoveries which I was later to make in Finland and in the western parts of the eastern area.   The barrel-vaulted churches of Spain recalled, as did S. Sophia at Sofia, the Mesopotamian technique of barrel vaulting.   In Dalmatia, however, another possibility occurred to me, owing to the presence of the blind arcades in the interior.

The inner wall pillars must have had a different function

originally from that of the blind arcades outside, since, particularly in the small one-aisled barrel-vaulted early Croatian churches, the pillars outside and inside do not correspond (Fig. 17). The inner pillars had originally a structural function. Later we shall see that the blind arcades outside are apparently a conventional survival. But the interior pillars occur in Finland, and in the frontier circle of Eastern Europe in contrast to the West with its long churches with block walls and raftered roofs. Plate XIV. (*b*) shows the Finnish block pillars, and Plate XV. (*a*) the structure of wall pillars in churches with a barrel vault of beams proper. If this relationship of the Croatian inside wall and pillars with wooden architecture is a sound theory, then the Croatians must have brought the technique of block walls and the barrel vault in all its forms from their trans-Carpathian home.

The Cupola.—If at the point where the roof begins beams are laid horizontally, and if the next beams are laid across the corners, the result is a cupola (Plate XV. (*b*)). The four beams lying over a square have then the shape of a rhombus superposed on the square. The next beams, laid across the corners of the rhombus, form a smaller square. Thus by alternate squares and rhombi we arrive at a pyramidal cupola.

Certainly this is not the only way of achieving by means of horizontal beams, roofs like those shown in Plate XIII. (*a*); but it may be, as I have shown in my *Armenia*, the oldest type. I cannot too often repeat that we are at the beginning of our researches in this field; perhaps the discovery of this new province of art-history may produce results of the highest importance. I can only record what I found in circumstances attended by great difficulties.

It was said in the first chapter that there is a marked difference between Croatian and Lombardic architecture. The Croatians use the vault from the beginning, while the Lombards do not. The reason may be, I think, the preceding wood architecture. The Slavonic Croatians being an Eastern people, built in blockwork; the Teutonic Lombards, perhaps, in framework. Therefore the South Slavs translated their roofs of true blockwork into barrel vaults and cupolas of stone, while the South Germans with their raftered roofs are satisfied with the early Christian basilica type which employs no vaulting. There is only one Teutonic race migrating to the South which seems, like the Croatians, to have built in blockwork before using stone materials and technique, namely, the Western Goths of Spain. This hypo-thesis can be justified by the fact that the Goths, before migrating to Western Europe, were settled for centuries on the Black Sea in the midst of the peoples using blockwork, and may have abandoned their earlier native German frame-work entirely.

Now the question is—What sort of block-building did the Croatians bring with them from their Carpathian home to the countries across the Danube and to the sea coasts ?

It seems astonishing that block-walled churches with raftered roofs should be vaulted and should appear in both types, with barrel vaults or with cupolas. I ventured to suggest the possibility of a wood origin for this kind of barrel vault. We may now compare the monuments with cupolas built with rafters, not with horizontal beams.

These are not less interesting for various reasons, the first being the mere fact of their existence. Whence arises the idea of building a cupola with rafters ? I had not given much consideration to these questions when I discovered this feature first in Finland (Fig. 25). It was there, moreover, that I heard the explanation accepted universally by scholars that these cupolas are merely copies of the usual Baroque cupolas of the time. But it was precisely these Finnish monuments that con-vinced me that this is a superstition. I saw quite plainly that in Finland, at that later period, the Protestant church designed mainly for preaching was quite naturally the origin of this sort of cupola. The type itself must be much older.

2. *Significance.*—Churches were not the first creations in wood and blockwork : there was a demand for them in the Christian era, and they looked to and carried on the traditions hundreds and thousands of years old, those of the ordinary dwellings in the east of the northern area. It is possible, however, that there was already in existence, in pagan times, a type of building with the same purpose as the church, to serve as the house of God and, at the same time, the assembly room of the community.

First of all we must look for pagan examples. We can now refer not only to literary sources, such as *Saxo Gram-maticus*, but also to the temple of Svantevit in Arcona (Fig. 34). It was a building with square walls and four pillars inside, all of wood. But what was the method of construction ? From a Slavonic temple one would expect blockwork. Then we should have a wood analogy in pagan times to the Croatian square church in ſtone with four pillars and to the same type in Armenia. In the fourth chapter, however, we shall find that the square with four maſts is also a leading type in Teutonic

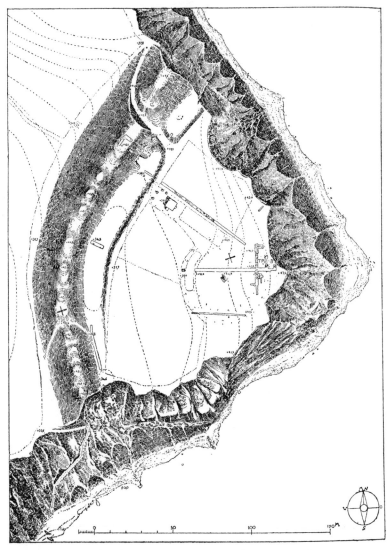

FIG. 34.—THE AREA OF THE TEMPLE OF SVANTEVIT IN ARCONA.

architeĉture. The raw material (wood) is the same, but the technique is notably different. It is scientifically impossible to assume that the temples of Rügen bore any relationship to the Teutonic temples, halls, or ſtave churches : these were probably rather akin to early Slavonic churches.   I shall not touch here on the question of statues with three or four, or even as many as seven, heads.   One monument of this kind still exists, and is in the possession of the Academy of Cracovia ; a *triglav* was also found in the ruins of Bribir in Dalmatia. We may recall, too, the old wooden church in the Silesian Smograu, where the Christian cult superseded that of the pagan Smok.   Similar pillars with human features stand in the centre of the Slavonic temples.   We are led to think that the square form is better adapted to liturgical requirements of this kind. In the German town of Brandenburg there is a model of an old church of S. Mary (Fig. 35), destroyed in the last century, which seems to have copied in stone in the twelfth century a wooden temple of Triglav, built in 982.   It is significant that the model shows " a very singular central building looking like a Byzantine domed church."   Does this show how the Slavonic peoples built their pagan temples ?

I noted in Finland the way in which new liturgical require-ments give rise to new architectural forms.   There the old Catholic Church type was not suited to the needs of the Protestants, who placed special importance on preaching. They desired, above all, a church in which the preacher could be heard equally well in all parts.   The long church (Fig. 24) was suitable for the concentration of all eyes on the celebrant of the Mass.   For the Protestants it was not the altar, but the pulpit that was all important (Fig. 25).   ·The voice must be heard in the centre of the church, and from this need arose the importance of the centre of the church.   I showed that not only the cruciform type church, but also the cavity of the ceiling and the cupola has its origin there.   Was this the first time that such a purpose was served by a church built of wood ? Does not the type naturally recur if the centre of a block-building is the essential part, as, for instance, the statue of a god, or a fireplace ?

3. *Shape.*—At this point the question arises where the builders of block churches acquired the art of building them. It is the custom to assume that the missionary himself, or architects following him, built the first churches, and thus that the new and universal long church with one aisle and, later, the three-aisled basilica were immediately introduced, the wooden church being in every case a copy of stonework. It is one of the main objects of this chapter to show that this idea is a mere superstition, since it was not the long type, but

the round, for stone, and the square, for wooden churches which were originally the leading shapes in the North, until bishops and monasteries built their representative monumental buildings in the usual Roman or Byzantine forms.

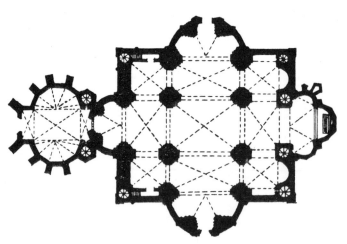

FIG. 35.—PLAN AND SECTION OF THE CHURCH OF S. MARY, BRANDENBURG (NOW DESTROYED).

Here we are concerned only with the square. We can now see why it is that all Slavonic church architecture in stone and in wood in early North European or pre-Romanesque times shows an inclination for the square form, and that while one Germanic people, for example the Goths, has this form while another, the Lombards, has not.   The former lived for centuries in Southern Russia, and introduced the system of block-building into Spain, while the Lombards, it would seem, originally built in technique similar to the West European framework.

The ground form of pure blockwork is the square with pyramidal roof.   The Croatians did not necessarily copy Armenian prototypes, but Dalmatian, as formerly Armenia may have been dependent on the eastern technique of block-building.   The most striking resemblance in shape between the two Christian art-streams in stone buildings preserved of the second half of the first millennium is precisely the fact that they begin with the conical cupola on squinches.   I showed in my work on Armenia how both shapes have their origin in the old Indo-Aryan block architecture, and it is tempting now to come to the same conclusion about the early Croatian church building in stone.   There, too, the squinch would be the translation into stone of the beam across the corner.   In the same way the conical stone cupola could be explained as derived from its pyramidal wooden counterpart.

The cruciform type with an open square in the centre, so much favoured by the Croatian church builders, is the standard shape for block churches with five cupolas.   We have seen the rich varieties that exist of this type, and it seems easy to find for every early Croatian form a corresponding type in wood architecture.   I myself wrote an article on one of these types which appeared in the *Revue des Arts Asiatiques*, 1927.

All these comparisons of cupolas, especially the conical cupola on squinches, refer to pure blockwork.   But there is, as I have said, the possibility that even in those early times the Croatians knew the technique of block-building with a raftered roof.   It is the long barrel-vaulted church with interior pillars that would be more nearly related to such a structure.

4. *Form.*—It is one of the main principles laid down in the history of art that wood architecture can never be monumental.   It is a temporary expedient, we are told, or a substitute, having no essential character of its own, and therefore the historian of art may neglect it, as in fact he does.   I hope that this state of affairs may soon be altered, if only scientific methods are employed, and opinions are not formed on a foundation of ignorance.

Anyone who knows what has been preserved in Europe alone of wooden churches will, as in the case of the Greek temple, see at once the fallacy of the art-historian. Wood architecture is essentially monumental, and we do not understand by this term great size only, as measured in metres, but rather the artistic criterion of the combination of mass and space, light and colours. The measurement in terms of metres is of secondary importance; a building of hundreds of metres may be less monumental than one reckoned in tens.

Here we are concerned only with blockwork, in which the material rather than the technique gives the form. An enormous mass of horizontal beams is used, which gives a heavy outside structure. Inside, a proportionate distribution of mass and space is a primary consideration.

It is an artistic principle in wood buildings of pure block technique, that is to say, in buildings where walls and roof are constructed with horizontal beams, that the square is always preferred. The Roman Church, with its timber-roofed basilica, had to overcome this predilection of the north on the frontier of countries that built in pure block architecture. In the journal *Slavia*, III., 1924, I showed a very interesting example in the earliest wooden churches of the West Slavs (Fig. 26). In the fourth chapter we shall see that the stave churches of Norway also begin, in my opinion, with the square, this original form being changed only owing to the influence of the Roman Church.

I had first to discuss this in my *Armenia*. There I was able to show that it may have been the Indo-Aryan migration that brought the square block-buildings with pyramidal cupola of horizontal beams in alternating squares and rhombs to the south. There, when translated into another material, into unburnt brick in Iran, into concrete in Armenia, and into stone in the Hellenistic countries, it became the familiar cupola on a square plan, first with squinches over the corners, later with pendentives. This Armenian square form is in every way a " monument "—more a monument, perhaps, than a church (Fig. 36 and Plate XX. (*a*), Mastara).

We may now turn to an example of a wooden block church in a poor village in Eastern Europe. Plate XVI. (*a*) and Fig. 37 show such a building in Wyschenka Welyka, in Galicia. Between the steeple to the right and the trees on the left we see a church of the square type with cupolas as at Chochoniow. It may have been built with an eye to monu-

PLATE XV

(*a*) Construction of Wall Pillars in Churches of the Finnish type with a barrel
vault of beams proper

(*b*) Cupola in Temple at Pandrethan (Kashmir)

PLATE XVI

(*a*) Church and Steeple at Wyschenka Welyka (Galicia)

(*b*) Church at Chochoniow (Galicia)

mental effect (Plate XVI. (*b*)).   I saw examples in wood in America ; this is the essential feature of buildings in the "c o l o n i a l   s t y l e."

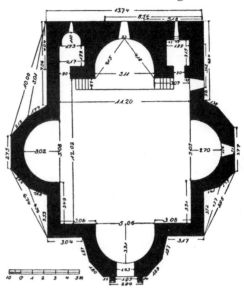

Wooden churches such as that of Hartford, Mass., produce the s a m e   m o n u m e n t a l effect as the achievements of the peasants of the Carpathian mountains built without columns of any kind. Such details, too, as the cupola with the lantern, a characteristic Italian motive (Bielavce, Plate XVII.), can be removed without detriment to the monumental effect, which will not be destroyed by a cupola of the indigenous type (Plate XVI).

FIG. 36.—MASTARA (ARMENIA). PLAN OF CUPOLA CHURCH.

The square with the cupola is in itself perhaps the most monumental form known to us. But apparently the proportions are satisfactory only by reason of the natural relation of the wall and roof in the single square, and the combination of three or five of these cupola squares in a line or in the form of a cross. In all these types, whether the central cupola alone appears between the gables of the adjoining roofs, or whether all three or five cupolas alternate, the impression is always monumental.

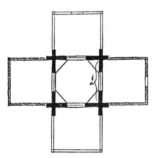

FIG. 37.—CHURCH AT WYSCHENKA WELYKA (GALICIA).

I now search for structures which can only be explained by the nature of the material and by the requirements of the blockwork and the shapes to which it naturally gives rise, such as the square with pyramidal cupola or the open central square with cross-arms from the four sides. The typical construction is that shown by Plate XVIII. (*b*). Is there any

further development possible? There is, as we shall see if
we look at Plate XVIII. (*a*). There we have the outside of
an apse, and we see that it termin-
ates not in a right angle (Plate
XVIII. (*b*)), but in an angle of 135
degrees. Figs. 38 and 39 show
ground plans with an apse ending
in three sides of an octagon. Now
let us conceive of a builder or
founder planning a building with no
square, but with angles of 135 degrees. There are two examples from
Finland, one (Fig. 38) a long church
(Kylmäkoski) with the two ends of
apsidal form, the angles being 135
degrees; the second larger example
(Westanfjerd, Fig. 39) being of the same type but with other
angles; and the other (Fig. 40 and Plate XIX. (*a*)) a cruciform church of that kind (Ruovesi). I do not think that
blockwork walls can show a greater individuality of treat-

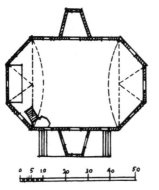

FIG. 38.—PLAN OF THE CHURCH
AT KYLMÄKOSKI (FINLAND).

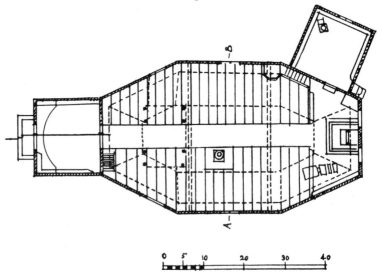

FIG. 39.—PLAN OF THE CHURCH AT WESTANFJERD (FINLAND).

ment. By this method of construction the effect of the roofs
is rendered most impressive, if they are built not with simple
gables, but according to the line of the walls with angles of
135 degrees and roofs, as shown in Figs. 38, 39, and 40.

PLATE XVII

Church at Bielavce (Galicia)

PLATE XVII

(b)

(a)

Details of Timber Construction in the Church of Nizhy Abscha (Galicia)

It is an astonishing fact that these structures are to be found not only in Finland, but at the same period—the eighteenth century, for example—in Moravia. Plate XIX. (*c*) gives a plan of the church at Velike Karlovice. It is undoubtedly the same form. How can this uniformity be explained? The humanist says that both churches, the Finnish and the Moravian, are copied from a Baroque model in vogue at the time. But is this possible? I hope my readers from their own observation will form the opinion that it is not. I am convinced that those blockwork forms were not found as late as the eighteenth century, but that they were already known in what are called the Dark Ages of European art, the pre-Romanesque period. We must not consider this period devoid of art. It had art of another kind, and, in particular, a flourishing wood architecture. In this chapter I attempt to give some idea of the eastern blockwork, tracing it back from later times. Woodwork, unlike stone, has not the virtue of being in favourable conditions imperishable.

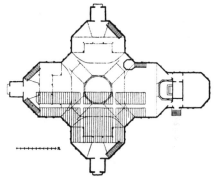

FIG. 40.—CRUCIFORM CHURCH AT RUOVESI (FINLAND).

The Catholic and Protestant cupola churches in Finland and in the Western Slavonic countries, whose roofs are built not with horizontal beams, but with rafters, have one cupola only. Their appearance and proportions are, therefore, entirely different. They were not built originally with the cupola, but with barrel-vaults; and the cupola in Finland is merely the result of the intersection of the barrel-vaults to make a dome over the chancel.

A good example of formal transition from wood to stone seems to be the blind arcades, which we have seen in early Croatian churches. I had already studied the question of their origin in Armenia. Now, with the hypothesis in my mind of Armenia surrounded by wood building, I can conceive of a wooden architectural motive, the embowered arcade, being in stone architecture projected flat on the surface of the walls.[1]

---

[1] Cf. the new journal, *Armeniaca*, I.

5. *Content.*—A wooden monument is the creature of a day. It is here to-day and gone to-morrow. Eventually it is burnt down or rots. It suggests a different individuality from stone. Wood building, especially if it is ponderous like blockwork, is not a particularly individual art form, nor is it personal. Blockwork is still at the present day Slavonic, as at the same time it is Finnish, and it must once have been common to all the Indo-Aryan peoples in Eastern Europe and Hither Asia as far as Iran and India. This community seems to me to be one of the most important facts about block building. It flourishes throughout the countries of the East, as does framework in Western Europe, and especially in England. You can see from the old wooden houses of England and those of Holland, Northern France, or Germany, the individual character of this branch of architecture. It was appropriately characterized in the year 560 by Venantius Fortunatus (cf. my book, *Der Norden in der bildenden Kunst Westeuropas*, pp. 103 *seq.*).

One feels that Slavonic block-buildings have in general an appearance of melancholy, of dull resignation, and pessimism. This, I think, is the last thing that could be said about western framework building.

III. Importance of the Monuments from the Point of View of Evolution.—We may now seriously consider the theory suggested by the Croatian monuments and other artistic products of northern peoples who migrated to the South, namely, that the great wood architecture of the North, the disappearance of which constitutes one of the greatest gaps in the history of art, may furnish a key to the pre-Romanesque church types of the Germans and Slavs. We have formed some impression of the wooden churches of Eastern Europe, although they belong to the last few centuries, and not to the period which concerns us, from the sixth to the eleventh century A.D., the Dark Ages. There are from five hundred to a thousand years between the two groups, the early North European or pre-Romanesque stone churches, and the types of wooden churches which I have been describing. Is it at all possible to work back from these late monuments to the period which in the first chapter we took as our starting-point?

1. *Constant Elements.*—The chief reason for the existence of wood architecture, in particular, blockwork for the period with which we are dealing in this chapter, is the presence of an extent of forest no longer found in Western Europe. In

Finland, the greater part of which is still forest, I could form some impression of it.   Building in wood is general in Finland to-day only by reason of the apparently limitless area of forest.

It seems to me that we must make this assumption for all other countries in which the highly developed blockwork building flourished in the last few hundred years, of which we have seen and discussed several church types.

If this primary condition, the existence of the forest, was fulfilled, it seems possible that the art continued during many centuries.   I do not believe that the houses of the peasants differed essentially in shape and construction from those of to-day.   Moreover, all the church types which we could definitely attribute to the last few centuries were in existence centuries before, and, it may be, were not a Christian development, but existed in pagan times.[1]

The first constant element in this kind of architecture is the raw material and its technique.   This alone in the case of block-building led to such forms as the square with the cupola.   I did my utmost to prove that in the earliest West Slavonic stone churches the square was used in the beginning in imitation of the earlier churches with blockwork walls.

This question of evolution has also been dealt with by Polish scholars in the *Spravozdania Komisyi do badania historyi sztukiv: Polsce*, VII.-IX.   One school, the humanistic, is convinced that wooden churches are imitations of Western European stone types.   They place at the beginning the most elaborate examples of the five-cupola type.   The opposition is represented by M. Obminski, who says that the simple square was the first stage and that all the more elaborate types were evolved from it.   In my *Armenia* I felt obliged, working, as I hope, from positive evidence, to begin with the square and to trace the development in Kashmir, India, Iran, and Armenia to the richest specimens which are found in Santa Sophia at Constantinople, and S. Peter's at Rome.

2. *The Influence of the Ruling Prince.*—In my work on the early Christian art of Asia Minor I attempted to prove that it was not Rome, nor Byzantium, nor the other great cities of the Mediterranean such as Antioch, Alexandria, and Carthage, that originated the new ideas in art.   The historians of art have made the creative power of the great cities an article of faith.   I was able, however, to show that many of the new

[1] Cf. Strzygowski, *Der Norden in der bildenden Kunst West Europas*, 2nd Edition, 1928.

architectural forms of Christian times had their origin in distant places in the East. In the large cities those eastern forms appear in a new guise on account of the larger scale on which they were reproduced, their precisely calculated structure and their splendid ornament. The will of emperors or churches and educational ideals could not of themselves create, they could but use what had been produced elsewhere, often in far-distant countries, by the persistence of situations, region, and race (cf. my article in the journal *Byzantion*, I.).

We can now observe the same conditions in the early North European art of pre-Romanesque times. What I pointed out in dealing with the cupola on a square plan in Asia applies also to Europe, in that the germs of the mediæval styles, developed on a large scale first by bishops and monks, and later by the cities, grew up from an area cultivated in the North by the Germanic and Slavonic peoples, and productive of wood art in all its forms. I must repeat that I exclude in this chapter what is called in the narrow use of the term, Western Europe. In the next chapter I hope to show the effect of the framework technique in wood, later on stone and brick architecture. In the present I am concerned only with the blockwork wooden architecture of Eastern Europe. We now know what led to its adoption by those in authority.

As long as the building was ordered by dukes and kings or bishops of individual countries (Croatia, for example) who were identified in their feelings with their Slavonic peoples, architecture continued along those lines, the essence of which is seen in the constant elements of the early North European art in wood. But as soon as the fiat of the Pope—later, of a Hungarian king—was given, the Croatian people ceased to be an outpost of early North European art, and became more or less an adherent of the art imported by church and court from Western Europe.

In the first chapter we found that the national unity of early Croatian art was at once destroyed when foreign kings and, in their train, Roman bishops and monks began to rule Croatia about 1105. The monumental stone architecture of Western Europe which we call Romanesque, Gothic, etc., took possession of the country between the bend of the Danube and the Adriatic, as it did in Spain and in the countries of the Western Slavs. The art which we call pre-Romanesque, or early North European, ended in stone building of a new

PLATE XIX

(*a*) Cruciform Church at Ruovesi

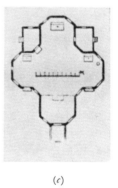

(*c*)

(*b*) and (*c*) Exterior view and plan of the Church at Velike Karlovice (Moravia)

PLATE XX

(b) Detail of a Wooden Mimbar at Kairwan, North Africa

(a) Cupola Church at Mastara (Armenia) West View

type.   The place of unhewn stone was taken by freestone in
the current international styles.   In Dalmatia it may be that
wooden churches were already becoming rarer on account
of the increasing scarcity of wood.   So much is clear.   But
what is not clear is the answer to a question which arises about
the Croatians from the facts gleaned from our knowledge of
the wooden churches of the East.   There is a frontier region
in the West, where the walls are built in the old blockwork
technique, but with a raftered roof imported from the European West.   This type, built half in framework and half in
blockwork, is particularly found in countries where the
influence of the Roman Catholic Church introduced the long
church, and put an end to the old square form.   Now the
Croatian people belong to the Roman Church : from the
tenth century the once Byzantine cities of the Adriatic coast,
and the opposition movement headed by the Bishop of Nin
in favour of a Slavonic liturgy, were in submission to Rome.
May not wood architecture have undergone a change at this
time ?   I shall point to the true answer.   I take as an example
the church of S. Peter in Priko, near Split (Plate III. (*a*)).
The design shows rafters over the vault.   If that were
correct, then the type of the wooden cupola hall must have
come under western influence.   But the design is wrong.
The architect designed rafters only because he could not conceive of another method of construction.   In Armenia and
in Dalmatia the early Croatian churches have the roof immediately above the vaults.   When I visited the monuments in
1924, I was able to assure myself that there also it was not
otherwise.[1]

　　3. *Effect of the Migrations.*—A document of importance in
research on wood architecture in the East in the first thousand
years of our era is the account given by the Byzantine Ambas-
sador Priskos of the Palace of Attila, in the country in which
the Croatians and the Lombards lived before they migrated
in the direction of the Adriatic Sea, the former to the East of
it and to the Balkans, the latter to the West coast and to Italy.
This account was written in 449 at a time when the Huns
were driving the Goths into Western Europe, as in later times
the Avars pressed upon the Slavs.   Who were the builders
of this palace of Attila ?   It can hardly have been the Huns
themselves, who were nomads and lived in tents.   I think

---

[1] Another example of the same kind is shown on Fig. 13.

that we may suppose it to have been built in the style of the Carpathian wood architecture, which is naturally blockwork. The description of Priskos gives, as might be expected, a round fortification (Fig. 41), but in the centre a German hall, the type of which we shall have to discuss in the next chapter.

We have ceased altogether to consider ornament, which in the first chapter was almost more prominent even than architecture. Is it because block-building had no concern at any

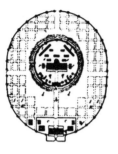

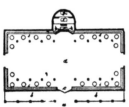

FIG. 41. — RECONSTRUCTED PLAN OF ATTILA'S PALACE.

time with ornament? As far as I can recollect, I saw no wooden church in the East with the abundance of ornament characteristic of the Hiberno-Saxon monuments of the British Isles or of the architecture of Norway, with which we shall have to deal in the last two chapters. I do not think that the wood carvings of Attila's palace, mentioned by Priskos as being on the outside, have any connection with Teutonic animal ornament. They may have been ornaments of the same geometrical patterns found on the Croatian stone monuments.

Plate XX. (b) shows a detail of a wooden mimbar in Kairwan, North Africa. It was imported in the ninth century from Bagdad, and may have been carved originally in some East Iranian country such as Afghanistan. The same band ornament of two and three striations is found on it as that described in the first chapter. It was not Attila and his Turkish people who introduced this type of ornament from the East, but rather those parts of Europe which had come under Iranian influence that probably provided the Huns with workmen to decorate the palace of their king.

CHAPTER III.

HALF-TIMBER CHURCHES IN WESTERN EUROPE.

THE difference between the east and the west of Europe, so far as wood architecture is concerned, lies, perhaps, in the fact that Western Europe from Roman times was not rich enough in forests to provide wood for the full-timber building of earlier ages, which in Russia, and still more in Finland, has continued down to the present day, not only in the building of houses, but also of churches. Single farms and entire cities which grew up in the northern countries of Western Europe, began to adopt a new style of timber building, half-timber, or framework. This is made up not of wood alone, but of a wooden frame filled in with other materials, such as wickerwork, clay, tiles, etc.; sometimes, indeed, with wood itself, cut in small pieces and occupying the spaces between the timberwork. The German name for this is *Fachwerk*.

This type of church is not usually mentioned in histories of European church art, but it must be studied, if art-history is to be founded on established facts and not merely on the orthodox theories of the humanists. In this chapter I hope to demonstrate that before the time of the great standard architectural styles, Northern Europe knew practically no other architecture but that of wood; we must therefore study the type. It is quite possible that the southern and south-eastern movement of stone building necessarily superseded the tradition of centuries in the North, and that certain motives, the origin of which was hitherto unexplained, may be regarded as concessions to the indigenous tradition of wood building. It is inconceivable that we can evade this problem, when we realize the influence of timber work on the development of vaulting, on churches built on the square plan generally, and, in particular, on churches with the cupola over the square: examples are forthcoming in the seventh century and in the Carolingian period in Armenia, with the Western Slavs, and in Dalmatia and Spain. As this type of architecture was not the

characteristic type in Western Europe, there is an *a priori* case
for the existence of another type of timber work.

In the east and south-east of Europe we have seen that
stone monuments imitated the earlier timber buildings.   In the
North and West, however, no such monuments exist.   How
then can we study the wooden monuments built in the second
half of the first millennium ?   No copies in stone or other
material exist, since wood was less scarce than in the South,
especially in the Teutonic countries.   It is known that in
Germany as late as 1050 wood was used to a greater extent
than stone, stone being used particularly for buildings built
to the order of the church or a ruling prince, or a monastery.
The popular style of building is indicated in the poems of
Venantius Fortunatus, the bishop who, in the second half of
the sixth century, travelled from Poitiers to the Rhenish
cities, in which he expressed his admiration of the wooden
houses which were the prevailing type.   In the British Isles
wooden churches were built in Anglo-Saxon times in a technique described as being *more Scotico*.

Before examining these facts in detail, it will be well to
state precisely the type with which we are dealing.   In
England the mention of half-timber churches suggests stone
churches with timbered towers.   In this short chapter we are
concerned only with true half-timber churches, and must leave
out of account all the picturesque towers with shingled spires
which lend the appearance of antiquity presented in towns by
half-timbered houses.   Both of these types are well known,
but the existence of half-timbered churches in England, as in
France and Germany, is not generally realized.   Yet it is
precisely those monuments of wood that are of the utmost
importance, which are found not only in twos and threes,
but, as in Brandenburg, Mecklenburg, and Pomerania, in
extensive areas with hundreds of monuments.   It is now time
to study these relics, as was done a century ago with the
mast-churches in Norway.   Only thus was it possible to
bring a few examples down to our own time, and it seems
likely that in England, for example, in the course of a few
years it will be impossible to find one genuine half-timber
church.

The orthodox view in England is that churches were
naturally built of stone, where it was present, and that where
there was no stone, bricks were used ; in the eastern counties
(Norfolk, Suffolk, etc.) flint and stone were the materials.

Occasionally timber arcading supporting a timbered roof may be seen inside the buildings, but one cannot call to mind any examples of half-timbered walls. In that case, it is thought the timber merely replaces and imitates stone ; it is, therefore, without interest for the art-historian. The present chapter is an attempt at least to question this view and to direct attention to the influence of the northern tradition on the mediæval monuments of the northern area of Western Europe.

I. The Monuments and Sources.—The extant half-timber churches all date from the last centuries. They are thought of as merely temporary structures, and, above all, as crude copies of stone churches, showing no monumental style or trace of an earlier origin. It must be pointed out, however, that in England itself—I do not speak of Ireland—timber work was beyond a doubt the only known technique for houses, halls, and the majority of the temples in pagan times. It must not, indeed, be forgotten that memorials to the dead and fortifications were sometimes built in stone in the North ; but the popular building material was wood. Documentary evidence is the first requisite for proving our case, by which we may fill the blank caused by the disappearance of the wooden buildings earlier than the sixteenth century by reason of the humidity of the northern climate. This question must be approached otherwise.

First of all we shall study the monuments preserved from the last few centuries, proceeding to the consideration of the mediæval documents which may throw light on the timber-work of England, France, and Germany. In this way we can bridge over the gap between modern buildings and the wood-work of the pre-Christian period, which will constitute the last section of the present chapter, dealing with the question of evolution.[1]

1. *Monuments.*—In examining the actual monuments, we shall proceed from East to West. In Eastern Prussia half-timber churches are found along with the Slavonic blockwork churches. German inventories of the monuments mention them, but do not give an exact description. The majority of these churches are built on a simple rectangular plan with a

[1] It is a matter of some difficulty in the absence of detailed measurements of the wooden churches. It was only with great trouble that I was able to obtain some plans and sections, especially in England. All that I could show was a few photographs secured for me by my publishers.

steeple at the west and an apse at the east end.   In the province
of Brandenburg are some examples dating from the sixteenth

FIG. 42.—PLAN OF THE CHURCH AT
FISCHWASSER (BRANDENBURG).

century.   A half-timber church in
a village called Fischwasser (Plate
XXI. (a) and Fig. 42) is of this
kind.   The wooden seats in the
church are dated 1600, the spire
1699 : the date of the building is
probably about 1600.   The steeple
is separate from the church ; the
half-timber walls support a heavy roof, and the general shape
is a simple quadrilateral.   The supporting and the horizontal beams of the walls meet at right angles, and only
in the lower part containing the windows are oblique beams
found.   In the church of Hermswalde, in the district of
Kossen in Brandenburg (Fig. 43), a small belfry rests on the

roof above an entrance on the south
side.   Here the half-timber work of
the walls is more elaborate, and diagonal beams appear in the rectangular
framework.   The chief feature of
interest is the apse, which is built in
the style of timber-work which we
have seen in the East, with the angles
of 135 degrees (p. 70).   In the illustration (Plate XXII. (a)) the walls
are seen behind the tree, and the

FIG. 43.—PLAN OF THE CHURCH
AT HERMSWALDE (BRANDEN-
BURG).

sloping roof over three sides of an octagon.   The interior
view (Plate XXII. (b)) shows the chancel and altar in the
apse and the walls covered with boards.   It is particularly to
be noticed that the roof is vaulted, and it will be observed
that the vaulting goes as far as the horizontal beam, at which
point it becomes flat.   At the apse end the vault is seen to

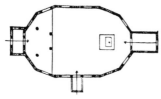

FIG. 44.—PLAN OF THE CHURCH AT
STORBECK (BRANDENBURG).

be constructed with boards nailed
to the frame-work of the roof.
The idea of an angular apse took
the fancy of wood builders, as
was evident in the full-timber
work of the East.   The half-
timber church of Storbeck (Fig.
44), dating from about 1730, and
another of the same type at Beutnitz, show a rectangular
plan with an apse at each end, the whole building being

PLATE XXI

(b) Church at Dirlammen (Hessen)

(a) Church at Fischwasser (Brandenburg)

PLATE XXII

(b) Interior of Church at Hermswalde

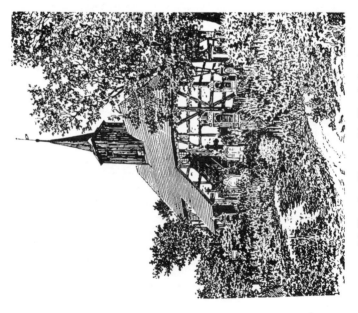

(a) Church at Hermswalde (Brandenburg)

PLATE XXIII

(*a*) Church at Wulfsahl (Mecklenburg)

(*b*) Rouen : Aîtres de Saint-Maclou

PLATE XXIV

(a) Warburton Church, Cheshire

(b) Besford Church, Worcestershire : Interior View

ten-sided.   Behind the altar of the Storbeck church is a
sacristy ; on the south side of the inner room, which is
9·66 m. broad, is a small entrance hall, another being found
on the west side before a gallery.

Plate XXIII. (*a*) illustrates a half-timber church at Wulfsahl
in Mecklenburg, and Plate XXI. (*b*) another at Dirlammen
in Hessen, which give a good idea of the northern and western
Teutonic types.

In the north of France, Champagne, Normandy, and
Brittany there are examples of timber churches.[1]   It is said
that the origin of the wooden churches of England can be
traced to this Continental group.   Those who have travelled
in the district of Seine Inférieure know that Rouen took the
lead in building private houses of half-timber work.   I can
only recollect the Aîtres de S. Maclou (Plate XXIII. (*b*)),
formerly a charnel-house of the sixteenth century.   Another
good example is the " Logis Adam " at Angers, illustrated on
Plate XXXIV. (*a*).   The tendency to diagonal beams in the
framework is typical.   Wooden churches are not found in the
towns.   Ypres was once rich in half-timber houses, and it
may be that in Belgium and Holland there are to be found
wooden churches dating from the last few centuries.

In England very few half-timber churches, in the strict
sense, have been preserved, and they have not been treated as
thoroughly and systematically as they deserve to be.   At a
time when a society founded for the purpose was taking steps
to preserve what remained of the mast-churches in Norway,
in England during the last hundred years these monuments
have been allowed to be destroyed.   Ignorant and thoughtless
restorers have had a free hand, with the result that now it is
almost impossible to find material for critical study and research.
In one book only,[2] as far as I know, is there a summary
account of English half-timber churches.   There are, indeed,
no plans and sections of the churches, which are in fact genuine
half-timber work ; but at least the book contains the names
of the churches with short descriptions.

The extant English wooden churches, with the exception
of Greenstead, which will be considered later, show clearly
that the technique of the English churches was half-timber

---

[1] I was unable to find in any library Tillet's *Les Eglises en bois de la
Champagne*.
[2] J. Charles Cox, *The English Parish Church*, London, 1914, pp. 256 ff.

work. They differ from the German churches, of which about 300 have a one-aisled interior which is but seldom found in the surviving English churches.

The church of Besford (*Frontispiece*), in Worcestershire, is a single-aisled church of this type, and has a foundation of stone, on which stand the walls of perpendicular and oblique beams, having at the west end and on the gable a few diagonal and curved beams ; on the west gable of the roof stands a small square belfry. The interior (Plate XXIV. (*b*)) is of interest, as it shows a tunnel vault. Dr. Cox [1] describes the church as a small building of rubble and plaster with timber framing, the nave apparently of the fourteenth century, and the chancel probably earlier ; at the west end is a square-headed two-light window with wooden tracery. A similar church is that of Melverley, Shropshire, with a single nave ; the walls are upright timbers with lath and plaster, dating from the fifteenth century. I fancy that in England, as on the Continent, it would be possible to find earlier examples of this type.

Another type is found in Cheshire, a county rich in half-timbered houses. In Plate XXIV. (*a*) the church of War-burton is illustrated. Dietrichson supposed that it dated from Norman times, but this theory was disproved by Meldahl, who assigned it to the fourteenth century. In 1891 he ex-hibited a model of it to the Anthropological Society of Vienna, showing three aisles under a single-gabled roof, and long walls with vertical timbers divided by a horizontal beam. Accord-ing to Dr. Cox,[2] the church was at one time entirely of timber, with timber arcading. Another church, Marton (Plate XXV.), a former chapel of Presbury, he says, was founded in 1343 ; it was of timber throughout, but considerably restored in 1850, and again in 1871, as is shown by the Gothic windows. The church has three aisles under a single roof. The frame-work chiefly consists of uprights, a short distance apart, banded together, as at Warburton, by a horizontal transom. On the west side is a porch with a square belfry and octagonal spire (Plate XXV. (*b*)). Inside are wooden arcades consisting of pointed arches which support the roof structure. The church terminates in a rectangular chancel. The best-known extant example of an old timber church is, according to Dr. Cox, the church of Lower Peover, but it must be remembered

---

[1] *Op. cit.*, p. 267.   [2] *Ibid.*, p. 270.

PLATE XXV

(*a*) Marton Church, Cheshire

(*b*) Marton Church : Detail of Steeple

(*a*) Lower Peover Church, Cheshire

(*b*) Interior of Lower Peover Church

that it was so largely rebuilt by Salvin in 1851-52 as to be almost a new building (Plate XXVI.). To-day the nave is divided longitudinally into three parts, each having a roof. On the outside of the walls are seen vertical and horizontal beams, the framework filled in with beams in rhomb lozenge form, between which are oblong windows. Inside the church we see in the main body of the nave four arcades on stone pillars, directly supporting the roof, to which there is no ceiling. The chancel is rectangular. Other churches are mentioned by Dr. Cox : " The church of Siddington (Plate XXVII. (*a*)), also a chapel of Presbury, in former times was originally of timber and plaster throughout. At present it is only the chancel which is of that construction, together with the south porch, and the belfry or square turret over the west end. At first sight the west front appears to be of an elaborate black and white design, but this is merely a bit of modern painting." Other remains of timber-framed churches in this county, and detailed descriptions of these above-mentioned, appear in an article by Dr. Cox in *Memorials of Old Cheshire*, 1910. The same author writes :—

" In Hampshire the small late-fifteenth-century church of Mattingley " [1] (Plate XXVII. (*b*)) " is entirely constructed of timber and brick. The body of the church is divided into *quasi* nave and aisles by four arches of well-moulded timbers, having side aisles which are but 6 feet wide ; the walls are composed of square beams of upright timbers with 7-inch intervals between them, filled up with diagonally placed thin bricks. In this county timber was freely used in church construction of the fifteenth century in the north-east and other parts where wood abounded.

" In Staffordshire [2] there are fine timber arcades in the church of Betley. At Rushton Spencer the church is supposed to have been built entirely of timber, and there are considerable remains in the interior. External half-timbered work also survives at Harlaston and Whitmore.

" Flaunden, Herts, used to possess a most picturesque timber tower in the priest's house adjoining, as shown in a drawing of about 1825. It gave way, alas ! to a modern church, which is claimed to be the earliest effort of Sir Gilbert Scott."

With a passing reference to the large half-timber church of Denton, a former chapelry of the once-great parish of

---

[1] *Op. cit.*, p. 265.   [2] *Ibid.*, p. 270.

Manchester, Dr. Cox concludes a summary, which he admits must not be taken as exhaustive. Probably more intensive research on the remains of half-timbered churches would yield additional evidence of the importance of this type of church building, as has been found in France and Germany, particularly in conjunction with the documentary and literary evidence.[1]

2. *Literary Evidence.*—The extant monuments of long and short work belong to the later centuries, the earliest preserved in England perhaps to the fourteenth : none is more than 500 years old. This fact alone explains the neglect by art-historians of such remains in England, France, and Germany. The first step to be taken to correct this view is to inquire into the documentary evidence of the existence of churches still older, and then to see if they were not of the same half-timber construction. The best answer would be given by a collection of the literary sources, of which only a few can be quoted here.

The most valuable evidence for the timberwork of the Rhenish peoples is found in the poems of the Bishop Venantius Fortunatus, whose residence was in the Frankish Poitiers and who visited the Rhine about 560. He thus describes the outside of wooden buildings :—

" Wall, built of stone, begone! I esteem higher the work of the craftsman in wood. In their mass the great timber palaces strike the sky, and in the firmly-built structure no chink can be seen. However sure a protection is stone, gravel, limestone, or clay, yet here a propitious wood has of itself built the house : higher it is and vaster, surrounded on all sides by a portico, and the builder has given free play to his fancy in the carving." [2]

In this poem on wooden houses, which were common in the cities of the Rhine, though not in Western France, the

---

[1] I must here refer to a communication kindly made by the Rev. A. Geyer of Glasgow, to the effect that there is a large number of wooden churches in Scotland, which, however, merely take the place of stone churches and are quite modern. The three volumes of McGibbon and Ross on *The Ecclesiastical Architecture of Scotland from the Earliest Christian Times to the Fifteenth Century*, 1896-97, make no mention of timber churches. They ignore the *mos Scottorum* quoted by the documents. The same limitation is found in the historians of early Christian art in Ireland, Mr. Stokes and others.

[2] Carm. IX. See *Monumenta Germanica*, IV., SS. ant., 219, Lib. IX., No. xv.

PLATE XXVII

(a) Siddington Church, Cheshire

(b) Mattingley Church, Hampshire

PLATE XXVIII

(a) Pirton Church, Worcestershire

(b) Warndon Church, Worcestershire

bishop is loud in his praise of the timberwork built of beams from the forests.   From the mention of the porticoes outside the walls we may infer perhaps that the houses stood free of one another; we see, too, that they were richly decorated. The question occurs to us—What type of timberwork is here described?

In another poem by the same bishop there is a description of the interior decorations of the houses :—

" Here in the room hang the glories of sculptured reliefs, and the fanciful images commonly shown by painting are wrought in wood.   The wall has received an adornment of figures, and what was once plain is now enriched by art."

While in other places painting in colour is found, says the bishop, here figures are represented in wood—a fact of some importance for our purpose.

Other writers, like Fortunatus, speak only in general terms of woodwork, and give no explanation of the technique. That half-timber work was known before the year 1000 is clear from excavations made in Frankenburg ob Rinteln, where walls from the ninth century are still extant, of from one to two metres in height.   There in the remains of a chapel were pieces of clay in great numbers, once used, it is fairly evident, as plaster for the wickerwork which filled the frames of the half-timber work in the upper parts of the walls.   The old castle building was destroyed by fire, and the clay hardened, showing that half-timber work must have been used.

The *lex Baiuwariorum*, speaking *de incendio domorum*, says : " *eam columnam a qua culmen sustentatur, quam Firstsul vocant . . .*[1] " This document says nothing about the walls, but it may be assumed that the roof was fixed on a single supporting beam. In Norway a type of church is found having a single mast erected at the point of crossing of two sleepers, supporting the gabled roof.   This is dealt with in the next chapter.   A supporting mast of this kind seems to be necessary only if the walls are not constructed so as themselves to support the roof.   Thus they must have been lightly built like those of the half-timber churches.   The question, however, arises—Was the " firstsul " a supporting beam ?   In Merovingian times wooden churches were built in France also, as we learn from Gregory of Tours—for example, at Thiers, Reims, and Tongres.   This last church was built *tabulis ligneis levigatis*. Wilfrid, the Scottish missionary to Germany, built, in 724, a

[1] *M.G.*, Leges III., 308.

chapel in Geismar from the wood of the oak of Thor (*ligneum oratorium*), the raw material (oak) suggesting, as we shall see, a half-timber church. There is a great deal of literary evidence of the Carolingian period for the existence of wooden churches. In one place only, however, in the description of the monastery of the island of Reichenau, is the half-timber technique suggested. This is the time, the ninth and tenth centuries, at which *quod primum de lignea materia initiatum, post hæc accuratiori lapidum structura . . . est perductum* (Würzburg, the Anglo-Saxon Bishop Burchard).[1] The houses of the monastery of S. Gallen were of wood plastered with clay until 1530. But as a general rule the wooden churches were replaced about the second half of the eleventh century by stone buildings. The best example is seen in Hamburg, where i.e. Bishop Unwan (1013-30) was, even at that time, building the entire city, including the palace and the church, in wood, while Bishop Bezelin (1035-43) rebuilt both of these main buildings in square stones. At that time a bishop took a pride in changing the technique, as we see from the *Vita Altmanni*, the life of the Bishop Altmann (d. 1091) of Passau, who came from Paderborn: " *Nunc operæ pretium est evolvere, ad quam uberem fructum terram sterilem vomere sani dogmatis Præsul Altmannus perduxerit, quam incultam, et sentibus plenam suscepit. Ante eius adventum omnes paene ecclesiæ in illo episcopatu erant ligneæ, et nullo ornatu decoratæ; immo ipsi earum presbyteri, ut ita dicam, lignei erant, quia coniugiis et terrenis negotiis dediti, divinis officiis penitus ignari, 'Miserere mei, Deus,' pro canone, 'Attendite,' pro passione legebant. Nunc autem ex eius industria omnes pæne ecclesiæ in episcopatu sunt lapideæ, libris, picturis, et aliis ornamentis decoratæ et quod maximum est, castis et eruditis viris bene munitæ. Insuper tota illa patria crebris coenobiis monachorum et canonicorum refulget, in quibus nocte ac die magna diligentia divinum officium fervet. Fama quippe eius opinionis adtraxit ex omni climate ad eum viros summæ religionis, quos perdiversa collocans monasteria, providit eis vitæ necessaria.*" [2]

This account recalls the introduction of the Roman Church 500 years earlier into the British Isles, when, after the first Irish-Anglo-Saxon movement in church building, the Roman teaching brought by S. Augustine gained the ascendancy. This mission saw the introduction of the stone church into England, the same thing happening later in Germany. We

---

[1] *M.G.*, SS. XV., 1, 56, lines 37-8.
[2] *Ibid.*, XII., 234, lines 26-36.

shall afterwards follow this movement step by step ; but for the present we consider merely the documents which show that before this Roman renaissance in England, timber was one of the principal materials in the building of the earliest Christian churches, and in particular that the half-timber technique was predominant.

The most valuable evidence is found in the well-known passage of the *Mirabilis Historia Ecclesiastica*, III., xxv., of the Venerable Bede, where he speaks of Bishop Aidan and the monastery of Lindisfarne : "... *ecclesiam ... more Scottorum non de lapide, sed de robore secto totam composuit atque harundine texit ... sed et episcopus ... Eadbert ablata arundine plumbi lamminis eam totam hoc est et tectum et ... parietes cooperire curavit.*" This took place in the year 582.

Bede refers to a certain type of timber building as being in the Scotic manner, that is to say, as practised in Ireland and Scotland, which was customary in his time. He goes on, however, not only to speak of wood-building in general, but also of hewn oak being used in this kind of wooden architecture. It will be seen later that this is a sufficient indication. The catch-phrase, *more Scottorum* appears again in other sources ; it is used in contrast to *more Romanorum*, which indicates building in stone, more particularly in quarried stone. I cite one other source only, referring to Saint Monene. She built a church *tabulis dedolatis iuxta more Scoticorum gentium*. Here is another hint as to the process of building *more Scottorum : de robore secto* and *dedolatis tabulis*. It might be translated, " from pieces of oak, with boards hewn off" ; it was possibly a combination of both.

We do not find this phrase *more Scotico* in other literary sources, only references to wooden churches. The account given by William of Canterbury, of the first Church of Glastonbury, is well known : there the walls were made of twisted osiers. The numerous other references to timber churches in England in the second half of the first thousand years of our era have been collected by Dietrichson in his work, *Norske Stavkirker*. I shall have to refer to it later, but at this point I do no more than quote the words of McGibbon and Ross.[1] " The practice of building with wood was the favourite one amongst the ' Scots ' in Ireland, and we shall find further examples amongst their disciples both in England and Scotland.

[1] *Op. cit.*, p. 6.

Dr. Reeves states that the ' Scotic ' attachment to wooden churches continued in Ireland till the twelfth century, and that although stone churches existed, they were regarded as of foreign introduction. These wooden structures, it is needless to remark, have all long since disappeared, having been replaced by more permanent edifices."

The nature of this " Scottish manner " will be discussed presently.

II. The Essential Character of Buildings in Half-timber Work.—There is a great difference between full and half-timber work in the matter of bulk, space, and proportions. This is not only a matter of raw material and technique, but more especially of the difference in spirit between the two. The northern mast-church, again, is entirely different from these in its essential character. The few and late surviving examples taken together with the documentary evidence help us to realize the importance of the early timber churches in England, France, and Germany. At this stage we must consider the characteristic features of these buildings and propound theories as to their origin.

1. *Raw Material and Technique.*—The wood chiefly used in half-timber buildings was, as Bede says, hewn oak. Eastern full-timber work uses whole beams of the several varieties of pine. The difference is thus very great, and is not only between horizontal and supporting beams. Apart from this consideration, building *more Scotico* must clearly have been framework. The question will arise later whether other kinds of wood, and consequently building with whole beams, were not found during the first millennium—in fact, the use of half and full-timber work side by side ; but for the present we may confine ourselves to half-timber work.

In considering the half-timber building we must distinguish between the outer walls and the construction of the interior. The walls are built of horizontal, supporting, and oblique beams, a frame which requires to be filled in with other materials. The illustrations which we have seen all show exteriors of this kind. There are buildings represented on panels of the Anglo-Saxon casket known as the Franks Casket in the British Museum (Plate XXXVII. (*a*) (*b*)), which seem to me to be possibly of this type, with horizontal and supporting beams and a curved roof. In the second illustration of this casket (Plate XXXVII.) is to be seen another building or throne in the representation of the adoration of the Magi.

This is of a similar type to that in the representation of Jeru-
salem, the two pillars supporting a curved roof being in each
case identical.

This type of wood building must certainly have been
known in the southern countries—India, Greece, and Rome.
It was known to Vitruvius, who speaks of the whitewashed
façade cracking; therefore, he says, only the panels are
plastered, not the wooden beams, both cracking differently.
This fact is familiar in England. The " old houses " and
country churches consist entirely of a timber frame filled in
with bricks on the outside, and inside with plaster. In some
of the rooms the horizontal and cross-beams can still be seen,
and the plaster. This is called " stud-work "; but in the
better rooms the stud-work walls are covered with "panelling"
—a carved wooden screen-work intended primarily to keep
out the cold, and secondarily for ornament. In the churches
the same scheme seems to have been followed in building in
Saxon times; but now there is a difference between the Continental and the English half-timber frame. In Germany and
France there is a predilection in favour of oblique beams
(Plate XXXIV. (a), Angers, le logis Adam), while in England
perpendicular supports are preferred, that is to say, very
narrow vertical beams with only a few horizontal (Plates
XXVIII. (a) and (b); Pirton and Warndon). If the well-
known English Gothic type of stone building has any relation to this type, we should have to prove by reference to
early wooden monuments that the type appears in wood earlier
than in stone. France does not appear to occupy an intermediate position between Anglo-Saxon and German; oblique
beams are common, while in Germany the oblique beams are
always found along with vertical and horizontal.

When *more Scottorum* is found in the literary sources, it is
only, or at least more particularly, the construction of the
walls that is meant. Dietrichson, whose work on the Norwegian stave-churches is, with all its faults, a perfect example of
what such a work should be, considers the church at Greenstead to be a surviving specimen of this type. This is not my
view, and we shall see below the class to which the church
belongs. The *mos Scottorum* is, in the opinion of Professor
Baldwin Brown,[1] a type of wood building peculiar to Keltic

---

[1] *The Arts in Early England*, II. (1925), p. 42.

tribes. He recognizes three essential forms of wood technique—the wattled hut, the block-house, and the structure of
framed timber work. I omit the first, but draw a sharp
distinction between the half-timber church and the stave or
mast-church. The one thing certain is that *mos Scottorum* can
refer neither to the stave or mast-church, nor to the blockwork buildings, since Bede speaks of " hewn oak." Therefore the probability is that to build *more Scottorum* means to
build in half-timber work. The evolutional problem attached
to this view is still unsolved.

Professor Baldwin Brown [1] considers that in the migration
period timber was so plentiful, both on the Continent and in
England, that the Teutons and the Norsemen did not trouble
to do more than cut down the number of logs required and
fit them together in the simple and solid blockwork manner.
To him it seems in the highest degree improbable that they
adopted the economical methods of later mediæval times when
wood was becoming scarcer, placing the uprights at long
distances apart, filling up the spaces with wattle and clay or
similar materials. It is possible that full-timber work and
pine forests were once general throughout the north of
Europe ; nevertheless, the economical half-timber work, far
from replacing the full-timber work in the later mediæval
period, seems to have been the prevailing style even in the
first thousand years of our era. When we come to deal with
the evolutional side of the question, I hope to make this clear ;
but in the meantime it should be pointed out that this point
can be settled nowhere better than in England, especially in
view of the term *mos Scottorum*. But, first, we must inquire
whether oak was always to be found in England, or if there
was a time at which pine-woods gave place to oak forests.

The scheme of the interior of a half-timber church on the
Continent consists of parallel upright frames standing one
behind the other. The lower part is open, and it is only
above the standing beams, which are visible outside, that there
are horizontal beams, which are seen from the interior. There
is a drawing by Jacopo Bellini (Plate XXIX.) which gives a
good idea of such a series of frames. Here we have only a
single nave and two additions, which are too small to be considered as side-naves. Among the surviving churches of the
last few centuries there are only a few examples of a three-

[1] *Op. cit.*, II., 198.

aisled church, as, for instance, the churches of Warburton, Marton, Lower Peover, etc., in England. I am uncertain whether this type is an old one in England or if in the much-restored churches the three naves are not merely due to the influence of the Roman basilica in later times, possibly even at the actual time of the restoration.

There are two types to be noted in the half-timber buildings in which the parallel frames are placed longitudinally. Originally each frame was independent of the others, as in Bellini's drawing (Plate XXIX.), but later, perhaps as late as the fifteenth or sixteenth century, they were bound together by beams at the top running round the entire building.

These questions cannot be settled by the restored English churches : an intensive study of the original structure is required. In England, possibly, there is a combination of early Norman influence with that from Norwegian stave and mast-churches.

One of the main features of half-timber building is the raftered roof. It seems to spring naturally from this technique, as it corresponds with the frames of the walls and the beams on the top, which connect them from the inside. It will be remembered that full-timber work employs only purlins, beams stretched longitudinally from one gable to another, or short beams in the form of a square across the corner. It is stated that the roof with horizontal beams (purlins) is also found in half-timber churches in England. There is no doubt that in England, as in France and Germany, the roof of the half-timbered church is ordinarily one of rafters resting on a horizontal tie beam and a vertical king beam, sometimes with a collar beam, struts, etc. I have not visited all the half-timber churches of England. In the reproductions which I have been able to show I find no confirmation of this theory.

The roof with rafters has on the Continent as far as Finland totally superseded the roof with horizontal beams on the slopes, with which we are more familiar in full-timber work. It is very interesting to observe that in all parts of the East in which the Catholic and Protestant Churches took the place of the orthodox Church, as in the case of the Western Slavs and in Finland, the long church with walls in full-timber work does not use the roof belonging to this type, as, per-haps, the wooden prototype of the Greek temple, but varies the technique of the roof using rafters. The effect of the

raftered roof is to give increased space inside the church by
substituting tunnel vaulting for the flat ceiling, as seen in
the East Prussian
church of Katz-
nase (Fig. 45).
It was a question
whether in full-
timber churches
this   type   of
vaulting   might
not   be   earlier
than   the   flat
ceiling, the pre-
ference for which
might have ap-
peared first in Re-
naissance times.
Here the Franks
Casket (Plate
XXXVII.) is of
importance.

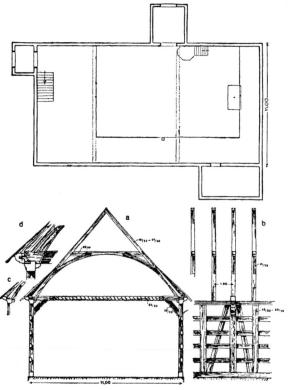

Vaulting
combined   with
rafters   is   pos-
sible, if, instead
of the tie-beam
and   the   king-
beam, collars
with angle braces

FIG. 45.—PLAN, SECTION, AND DETAILS OF THE CHURCH AT
KATZNASE, GERMANY.

are used as indicated in Fig. 46, a small triangle being formed
at the point of junction on each side.   In each case the vault
is made up of boards nailed on pieces of oak and placed ob-
liquely between the collar beam and the triangles.   These
vaulted roofs are found in genuine half-timber churches in
Germany.   I became acquainted with them more especially in
the mid-European region in which the eastern block walls
support a roof of rafters ; in Finland and in the countries of
the western and southern Slavs.   In England they may be seen
in early English churches such as Stow Bardolf, in Norfolk
(Fig. 46).[1]   There the rafters are placed on a stone wall, and
the nailed boards by which the tunnel-vault is effected can be

[1] Cox, *op. cit.*, p. 272.

PLATE XXIX

Drawing by Jacopo Bellini. *The Adoration of the Magi*

This drawing is a good illustration of the Continental type of timber-frame construction

PLATE XXX

(*a*) Interior of Marton Church, Cheshire

(*b*) Half-Timber Church at Vogelsberg, near Fulda (Germany)

readily visualized. Again, in England there is a definite preference for the open roof; although in the south-west are found waggon-roofs of the vaulted type, as also in the *Salle des pas perdus* of the Palais de Justice at Rouen, and in several places in North Italy.

There are many varieties of the open roof in England. Dr. Cox[1] has collected numerous illustrations of the two main types. To the one type belong the roofs at

Fig. 46.—Timber Roof at Stow Bardolf Church, Norfolk.

Marton and Nether Peover (shown on Plates XXV. and XXVI.). The other type, with well-marked tie-beams, may have affinities with that of Besford (Plate XXIV. (*b*)). It is, however, still premature to pronounce upon the relation of this preference for open roofs to half-timber churches and to the *mos Scottorum*.

The half-timber churches must be very carefully studied from this point of view. My experience on the Continent, in Scandinavia, and Finland has shown me that in many cases on new roofs traces are to be found of an older structure.

2. *Purpose and Significance.*—The wooden church surviving down to the present time was built by the peasant carpenter to be a centre of peasant life; it is thus distinguished from a wooden house in a city built by an architect. In the cities the wooden churches have entirely disappeared, being replaced by stone buildings. In the country, however, wooden churches and houses may still be seen in close proximity. They are built the one like the other. Plate XXX. (*b*) shows a church in Vogelsberg, near Fulda in Germany. The church looks like a simple house. It is quite certain that for centuries before the building of churches in half-timber work, houses were

[1] Cox, as above, pp. 274 ff.

built in this technique. Research in folk-lore should show that popular or peasant art might very well be studied in this type of house, were it not that owing to the dampness of the soil the lives of these buildings are a few hundred years at most. It must be observed, however, that the half-timber house was not the only kind of peasant building. I need only refer to the palisade house in Wales mentioned in a twelfth century statute law, a building divided into three parts with a roof consisting of the palisade beams bound together. The type illustrated by Marton Church may be related to it.

Here we deal only with churches ; but it may be repeated that in the British Isles half-timber work is particularly common in private houses, and not only in the country, some of the best examples appearing in the towns, even in London. We may recall the poem of Fortunatus, illustrating a specimen of such a house, and ask ourselves if, with the material that we have in England, we cannot form some conception of an early northern town of wood. They must, one fancies, have had a certain homely charm not found in the modern stone streets and squares, and it is refreshing to come upon an old half-timber house such as the " Dutch House " at Bristol (Plate XXXI. (a)) among the buildings of brick and stone. Then, too, originally the lowest storey of these houses could be built with arcades providing the type of covered walk mentioned by Fortunatus. It will be noticed that only horizontal and vertical posts are used, and that there are projecting portions on both sides. In some houses another characteristic feature is to be observed, namely, the projection of the upper storey beyond the lower, and windows closely grouped filled out with coloured glass sometimes replace the wall. This is well shown in houses at Langley, Kent (Plate XXXII. (a)) or in Germany in Hildesheim (Plate XXXI. (b)). Manor houses and large country mansions illustrate the same type. A very museum of all types of half-timber houses will be found in Cheshire.[1]

In some parts of Germany, especially in Hessen and Thüringen, in small towns, not only private houses but the town hall is built in half-timber work. One of the most picturesque buildings of this type is at Michelstadt in the Odenwald, in Würtemberg (Plate XXXIII.). The building

[1] Cf. The Studio Year Book, 1920, " The Furnishing and Decoration of Cottages."

PLATE XXXI

(b) Timber House at Hildesheim (Germany)

(a) The "Dutch House," Bristol

PLATE XXXII

(*a*) Rumwood Court, Langley, Kent

(*b*) Interior of Shenfield Church, Essex

is between two streets in the foreground and the church behind.   It consists of three parts, the ground floor, an upper storey with two octagonal corner rooms, and the high angular roof between two small pointed spires over the projections. This type is also used in the Harz towns, as, for example, in Wernigerode (where the town hall of 1498 is similarly situated), and in Duderstadt, where the type changed between 1432 and 1528.   Here the ground floor is of stone, but the open arcades remain, which are seen at Michelstadt in a wooden structure. Two pairs of cross-beams form the broken arcade and, in particular, the projecting corner-rooms are supported by other cross-beams.   These motives were also used in church architecture.   The question whether pagan temples and royal halls were built in half-timber work must be left for consideration to the last section on evolution.

3. *Shape.*—Half-timber churches were the work of carpenters, and the tradition did not admit of great variety in shapes.   A thousand years ago the shape was essentially the same as that of to-day.   The only change, perhaps, was in the position of the entrance.   Formerly these rectangular buildings had their entrance on the south side, and, as the church was broad in proportion to its length, the altar may have been in the middle of the long north side, opposite to the entrance. This was the tradition handed down from pagan times, but the Roman Church changed the northern system.   The new canon regarded the church longitudinally, placing the altar at the east end and the entrance at the west.   I first saw signs of this change in Armenia, and one of my pupils, Mr. Bruck, in a dissertation, noted the same fact in the half-timber churches of Northern Germany.   It is also to be found in England. In the church of Marton in Cheshire there is a good English example (Plate XXV.), the porch being placed on the long south side.   This is not an isolated instance.

The normal plan of the half-timber church in England is always rectangular, and it is immaterial whether the nave is broad or long, looking to the east.   It is a hall without an apse, the altar being placed against the east wall.

There are, however, exceptions.   Timber arcades are not unknown in half-timber churches.   In Germany, churches of this kind are seen with two naves, arising from the fact that the beams had to be supported if the breadth increased.   An English example of another kind is the church of Shenfield, Essex, which was built in the " Early English " period towards

the end of the thirteenth century. Originally it consisted solely
of nave and chancel; but late in the fifteenth century a chapel,
a north aisle, and a south porch were added. In making these
alterations it was found expedient to pull down the north wall.
A plan is given in *The Churches of Essex*, by G. Buckler (see
Fig. 47), and Plate XXXII. (*b*) gives an interior view. The
north wall is replaced by wooden arcades in oak. It is an
interesting example of Gothic pillars in wood, but does not
seem to have any bearing on early half-timber.

Two-aisled churches can be built in the true timber technique; but three-aisled examples are rare, and seem to be

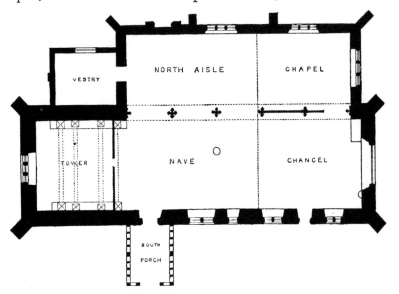

FIG. 47.—PLAN OF SHENFIELD CHURCH, ESSEX.

descendants of the Roman basilica. Such, for instance, are
the churches of Warburton, Marton, Nether Peover, etc.
(Plates XXV., XXVI.).

The most noticeable shape that has its origin in wood is
that of the apse. Rounded apses are natural to stone churches,
but rectangular apses, sometimes merely the end of the hall,
seem to indicate a wooden origin. In England the square east
end found favour. On the Continent we might point to the
Cistercian type, which has its origin in wood technique. This,
like the inclination to the perpendicular style, is another relic
of a former age when timber building was general in England.

Another type of apse is that which we have already seen in

PLATE XXXIII

Michelstadt (Germany) : The City Hall

PLATE XXXIV

(*a*) Half-timber House at Angers (Le Logis Adam)

(*b*) Detail of Galleries in the Market Place at
Mirepoix (France)

eastern blockwork churches, the polygonal apse of three or five sides of an octagon. From this type springs another, the church with two apses (Fig. 44). It will be recalled that in the east of Europe this form with angles of 135 degrees was much in favour; in Finland and Moravia churches still exist with four such apses. The question is whether this type had its origin in the East, whence Western Europe derived it, or whether it was also indigenous to the West at a time when full-timber work was known there.

Rooms with a small projection in the form of five sides of an octagon often appear in private houses; we may compare the Bristol house (Plate XXXI. (*a*)), and the town hall of Michelstadt (Plate XXXIII.). In Holland and England the type was familiar.

What was the ornament of the half-timber churches? Was it simply the pattern of the beams on the outer walls? These, with the walls which they enclose, have a very decorative appearance. Some students supposed that the beams could be made to form Runic letters, but there is no proof of this, and it is on the whole unlikely. It would, nevertheless, be interesting to give the main types systematically arranged. The specimens shown on Plates XXX.-XXXVII. gives some idea of the possible varieties.

The wooden beams themselves call for carving. There is a series of motives in Romanesque and Gothic art which might conceivably be imitations of old timber carving. Some motives of this kind are seen in a frieze of small arches cut on an outside projecting wall. Fig. 48 gives some motives of the kind.[1]

It would be of the greatest value if we could prove that the cube-capital has its origin in half-timber work. I do not think that this is so. Certainly in Armenia it exists to a great extent in the seventh century. Perhaps its origin is like that of the church with two apses.

Recalling the poem of Fortunatus, we are astonished to find no covered walks round the churches as we saw them in full-timber work and in the Norwegian stave and mast-churches. We know that they appeared in Western Europe, on the Continent from the town hall of Michelstadt, and also from France—for example, the galleries in the market-place at Mirepoix (Plate XXXIV. (*b*)).[2] The construction is the same

---

[1] Wesser, *Holzbau*, p. 13.
[2] Scheffler, *Der Geist der Gotik*, Tab. 59.

as in Germany, with similar cross-beams. In later times inscriptions, and religious and domestic scenes are favoured
for decoration, especially from the Renaissance. In the first
thousand years this is not to be expected, as representational
art did not appear, only ornamental motives. When Venantius
Fortunatus speaks of figure-reliefs, these must have been made
under the influence of Roman tradition.

England is fortunate in having preserved entire a series of
monuments which might be considered to be imitations in
stone of old half-timber buildings. The best-known example
is the tower of Earls Barton church, reproduced as an example

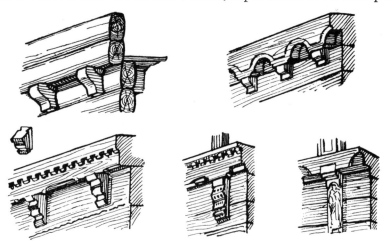

FIG. 48.—MOTIVES FOR CARVED BEAM-ENDS ON THE OUTER WALLS FOUND IN
GOTHIC AND ROMANESQUE ART.

of this in all art-histories (Plate XXXV.). On seeing it for
the first time from a distance, I was convinced that it must be
timber work. The upright posts connected in the lower parts
by oblique pieces cut from oak are characteristic of half-timber
work. More typical still of wood technique are the balusters
on the sides of the six windows : they have come from the
turnery. The best examples have been found in excavations
at Jarrow and Monkwearmouth, and in other Anglo-Saxon
churches. I mentioned these places in my *Origin of Christian
Church Art*.

Barnack (Fig. 49) shows another tower of half-timber construction imitated in stone ; there the old windows have no
balusters, and terminate in gables. They are closed with
panels decorated with two-striped band ornaments. My first

PLATE XXXV

Earl's Barton Tower, Northamptonshire

PLATE XXXVI

(b) Salzburg, Austria. A View of the City in 155

(a) View of Old Vienna, after Hoefnagel (1609)

(a)

impression of the imitation of wood architecture in stone was formed when visiting the church of Backwell, near Bristol. The form is that of a three-aisled basilica, but characteristic details appear on the dividing arches and the door. The Anglo-Saxon church of S. Pancras at Canterbury seems in the three entrance halls to preserve the typical arrangements of a wooden church.

4. *Form.*—The appearance of the half-timber church of to-day is not particularly striking. But at one time not only private but also monumental buildings were of wood and in this technique, that is to say, again during the period before stone architecture was for the second time introduced into the British Isles by

FIG. 49.—BARNACK CHURCH, NORTHAMPTONSHIRE.

J. Johnson, *del.*

the Roman Church. The question arises whether certain artistic qualities in Anglo-Saxon and Norman churches, as for instance, at Durham, and later in churches built in the early English style, may not have been inspired in some of their features by wooden precursors. It is incorrect to

deny monumental quality and the possibility of an evolution
of styles in the wooden architecture; the term is relative
according to the period in question.   It is not a mere paradox
to say that all " architecture " has its origin in wood building,
and originates in the North.   Stone building came from the
South, where the initial stage was rock-cut buildings and
caves : only the carpenter had, as it seems, from the beginning to join together single pieces to construct a building in
the open with an interior room.

The characteristic feature of a half-timber church is the
longitudinal orientation, while that of the full-timber building
is to focus the attention on the height, over a square plan.
It is the same contrast as we observe in the catch-phrases
" basilica " and " central."   In wood architecture the full-
timber work is not the only representative of the square plan :
the mast-church, as we shall see, was also originally built on a
square.   Half-timber, on the other hand, never inclines to the
square, but always to the rectangular form.   That is the point
in which it is not distinguishable from the basilica, where,
however, the nave is in three parts, the peasant building having
one nave only.   This is the general view, and the point requires
some investigation.

The Christian Church is imagined as a long building with
the entrance in the west and the apse in the east.   But, as we
saw, we shall have to consider the somewhat novel idea that
the half-timbered church may have been at one time viewed
as a broad building like a Chinese temple, with the main or
only entrance on the south side (cf. my *Der Norden in der
bildenden Kunst Westeuropas*, pp. 210 f.).

Bulk.—The æsthetic effect of a half-timber church depends
upon the proportions of the wall and roof, the combination
with the tower, vestibules, and particularly upon the apse ;
the building, as a whole, has a prismatical appearance, due to
the compact ensemble of roof and walls.

The rectangular form of a half-timber church with raftered
gables at both ends is different from that of the true full-timber
church with two heavy gables supporting horizontal roof
beams.   This difference gives the contrast between the architecture of the Greek temple type and the half-timber church.

The walls of a half-timber building show the evolution of
a definite building technique.   On a stone wall it is inevitable
that the scheme of construction cannot be seen, but in half-
timber work the system is necessarily visible.   It is quite

possible that here also are some traces of the beginning of the Gothic buttresses. It is clear how the beams are joined together, and built so as to conſtitute a ſtrong and ſtable scaffolding. In this syſtem are the germs of many architectural forms, and it seems possible that when half-timber technique was at its higheſt point, all these forms had been discovered and brought to perfection. All the beams have their purpose, and are adapted to practical ends. Here we have the materia¹ ; for the creation of a ſtyle, and it is unfortunate that we cann· make any definite ſtatements, that we can only propouna theories from ſtone architecture and some apparent survivals in wood buildings of recent centuries. All wooden monuments of mediæval times on the Continent and in England seem to have disappeared.

There is no sign of such a syſtem in the walls of a full-timber building, although a transition to it seems to be suggeſted, for example, in Finland, in the block pillars of the walls with horizontal beams combined with raftered roofs (Fig. 24).

There is, however, in Norway a third and very remarkable interior scheme of conſtruction which, along with the wall syſtem of half-timber churches, originated another movement towards a conception of architecture as an organic whole.

Space.—The appearance of a timber church in the landscape and the effect of its interior should, as in a Chinese temple, be related. Once the church added to the beauty of the landscape and was merged in it, although to-day many of them are surrounded by great trees. They are grateful spots in the landscape on which the eye may reſt. It would be intereſting in ſtudying these half-timber ſtructures to show their influence on town-building and the appearance of the architecture on the landscape. It is an illuminating fact that Vienna ˊof the present day, judged by the predominant ſtyle of its monumental architecture, is a Baroque city ; but a visitor passing through the ſtreets and squares of the actual city, the " Innere Stadt," will at once be ſtruck by the contraſt between the Baroque houses, palaces, and churches, and these narrow rooms, which seem to be a relic of an older world. They are, in fact, the rooms of the old wooden town, where the gable was the portion of the house facing the ſtreet, not the broad front and roof as the scheme of the Italian town requires. Plate XXXVI. (*a*) shows a view of old Vienna drawn by Jacob Hoefnagel in 1609. The difference is clear between the city as it was then, and its state before the counter-reformation, when monastic settlements and the new nobility from Italy, Spain, and France changed the old national character of Vienna. Another good example of an old drawing (1553) of a town is that of Salzburg (Plate XXXVI. (b)). In reality the streets are very narrow; in the view given they are made very much broader. All the houses have their gables turned to the street, but they are in groups of two, three, and more, surrounded by a wall ("Grabendach").

The only survivals from that earlier age in Vienna are a few Gothic churches, notably the church of S. Stephen; the other buildings, palaces, and houses have entirely changed. The narrow streets and squares are the only reminder of the old Gothic time. What of the old towns of Germany, France, and England?

The interior aspect of a half-timber church is somewhat of a contrast to the impression given by the outside. Light is thrown on the question of this inner room by the fact that the interior of a half-timber church consists of a single-aisled nave; other examples are found of half-timber churches with two aisles, but they are exceptional. The three-aisled church seems to be derived from the southern basilica. It is true that one or two lateral additions to the main nave are possible, as the Bellini drawing (Plate XXIX.) shows, but the typical form is the undivided nave without the side portions. The important work remains to be done of taking detailed measurements of all the interiors of surviving half-timber churches, and comparing the dimensions and proportions with those of Anglo-Saxon, Norman, and Gothic stone churches.

Another important point that concerns the evolution of mediæval church architecture is the question of proportion in relation to vaulting. Had the earlier wooden churches—in particular, the half-timber churches—a vaulted ceiling, or are the vaulted ceilings in the later wooden churches merely imitations of stone roofs? On the answer to this question depends deeply the whole feeling of space in the interior. I illustrated the half-timber church af Katznase, in West Prussia (Fig. 45), a vaulted building of this kind. It is a plain rectangular hall with a wooden barrel-vault reaching to the first horizontal beam in the framework of the roof. The roof consists of nailed boards, and it is a question whether such a structure can be considered a vault. But, as I point out on page 55, there are true vaults in wooden churches, and the churches of the province of Szathmar, for example, show that long churches of blockwork can be vaulted, not with nailed boards but with beams. Another blockwork church with a raftered roof is found near S. Veit in Carinthia (Plate XII.).[1] Whether this construction is seen in half-timber work I do not know. It seems to me impossible.

Light and Shadow.—The most striking feature of this kind of building is that the walls could be open, if that were desired. I know of no wooden church in which this was so, but it may be that, as in the case of private houses, the effect of this quality which underlay half-timber work became clear only in later times in buildings made in other materials. It is, for instance, typical of half-timber houses that they show an abundance of windows. That seems to suggest a possible reason for the open wall of a Gothic cathedral.

The covered walks surrounding the ground floor of half-timber houses gives an effect of light and shadow, which is specially noticeable in the streets and market-places of cities. We are inclined to call this an Italian fashion, on account of the translations into stone seen in towns such as Padua and Bologna. But its first appearance is in wood, as we see from the description given by Fortunatus, in which he contrasts the walk round the wooden Rhenish houses with the houses of his own Romanized country. Plate XXXIII. shows the high artistic value of the contrast between the upper floor and the ground floor with its dark opening, where the arches of heavy beams seem to frame dark masses.

Colour.—The façade of a half-timber work building, with the natural brown to black of the beams offset by the white-washed panels, gives a contrast of design and ground which produces a fine effect of colour; the appearance of a small town composed of such buildings would not easily be forgotten. The pleasing impression created by the colour of wooden houses is known to us from Scandinavia, and literary sources attest the beauty of towns built in half-timber work, as, for example, the description of Vienna given in 1444 by Æneas Sylvius Piccolomini, afterwards Pope Pius II. The effect of the interior of the wooden church must also have been colouristic, to judge from the private house and the Gothic stone church. Is it possible that the feeling for colour in

---

[1] *Slavia*, III. ; *Der Pflug*, I.

chiaroscuro had its origin in half-timber churches with windows instead of walls, and in houses like that shown on Plate
XXXI?

5. *Content.*—Wooden churches at the present day suggest
a rustic community, but at one time in the North they were the
form of architecture characteristic of the whole nation. The
high culture of the South in Roman times regarded wood as
an inferior medium, to be used only for humble buildings.
That was not the feeling of the North. Stone building was
introduced in the North first by the Roman Empire, and again,
later, by the Roman Church. In the meantime, the first
Christianization of the British Isles was based on national
customs so far as church building was concerned. Later on,
when Christianity had made a second appearance, building in
wood was known as *mos Scottorum.* It is similarly the national
factor that is to be looked for in the north of France, Belgium,
the Netherlands, and Western Germany; in Eastern Germany
half-timber churches are in the nature of a colonial style; the
type was brought from the West, as was full-timber work from
the Eastern countries.

Dwellers in such towns as the old Vienna (Plate
XXXVI. (*a*)), or in half-timber streets and squares (Plate
XXXVI. (*b*)), where a wooden church instead of a stone
church must be imagined, must have felt more at home in
such surroundings than in towns built in the new imported
styles by court, church, and monasteries. There is a suggestion of peace and contentment about a half-timber house, and
the same is true, as far as my observation goes, of the churches.

What influence, if any, had half-timber work on decorative
art and ornament itself? The monuments of this kind
which survive present no certain basis for an answer; but
we may suppose that at the end of the pagan period purely
ornamental or symbolic motives, and not representative figures,
were employed. The influence of the Mediterranean area in
Roman and Christian times changed this taste.

**III. The Importance of Half-timber Churches from
the Point of View of Evolution.**—Conventional art-history
confidently asserts that these churches, like those of full-
timber work in the East, are of no importance. The common
belief is that they also were built solely in cases of necessity,
and were then imitations of stone churches. If, however, we
believe that all domestic architecture before the middle of the
first thousand years of our era, and all churches not owing

their origin to Rome, in Germany down to the middle of the eleventh century, were of timber-work, then we must ask ourselves if, while we have lost the remains of all the early monuments, we may not have preserved their types. This problem at once shows the importance of studying the extant half-timber churches of recent centuries ; even if no mediæval church is left, possibly the types may have survived in these buildings. A new complexion is put upon the problem of these churches if we regard them as the last survivals of a vanished culture of purely northern character ; we may find in them features deserving of serious study. Are not the types far older than the actual churches, and are they not suggested by them ? Above all, we must remember the prevalence of these churches in the early centuries of the Christian era in the North, of which the extant churches, though of recent date, give an idea.

The mere possibility presents the history of art in a new light. If the wooden buildings of Western Europe are of real importance, if the surviving half-timber churches were no mere imitations of stone buildings, but even their precursors in the Middle Ages, European art would seem to be derived from an art-stream which was active not only at the beginnings of the Greek temple and the Indo-Aryan cupola on a square plan, but also at the introduction of Christianity into the North with its new purpose for buildings.

Framework is used throughout the western part of Northern Europe, on the Continent, and in England, but is not common in Scandinavia. It seems quite possible that the full-timber work of Eastern Europe was once general in the West also, but that with the destruction of the forests a new technique calling for less wood had to be employed. The first question which presents itself is whether the substituted technique is indigenous or of foreign derivation. Were there constant forces at work in the North itself, or was southern influence present ? The countries west of the British Isles, with America in the far West, were still unknown lands : Europe was, to all appearances, cut off from them as by a wall. The new technique is not of the north or north-east : it is to the north of the Continent itself, or to influence from the South that we must look.

An important point bearing on the evolution of this technique is the date at which half-timber work appears in the north of Western Europe. As it is mentioned by Vitruvius, it muſt have been known in Roman times, and the natural supposition is that it was introduced into the North of Europe by the Romans. That is conceivable; but the true reason why full-timber work was superseded by half-timber was the increasing scarcity of foreſts, and it is certainly possible that the Weſt of Europe itself originated the new method of building.

Again, we muſt inquire at what period half-timber work was at its height in Weſtern Europe. Was it in the time of Fortunatus—that is to say, in the sixth century—or rather about the middle of the firſt thousand years of the Chriſtian era? That was the date of the Song of Beowulf, with its description of the Heorot's hall, and the account given by Priscus of the palace of Attila. Possibly, too, it had not begun to wane at the time of the introduction by the monasteries of ſtone architecture, when southern builders had to inſtruct the northern craftsman; these may in turn have been influenced by the ancient half-timber tradition, which served in the North for buildings of all sizes and types, and particularly for those of monumental size.

The remainder of the chapter will be devoted to an attempt to prove that half-timber work is of North Continental origin, to an examination of the influences which hindered or deſtroyed its free evolution in church architecture, and, laſtly, to a ſtudy of the hiſtory of this once all-important raw material, its technique and artiſtic values.

1. *Conſtant Forces.*—In winter the northern peoples are pre-occupied with the problems of shelter and clothing. These needs ſtimulate handicraft, and it is from them that art in the North is derived, not, as in the South, from the desire of a ruler to impress his subjects. In the firſt thousand years of our era the Teutonic peoples changed the face of the ancient world. We are ignorant of the buildings and ornament of the Eaſtern Teutons, who firſt left their countries on the Baltic and on the Black Sea, their places being taken by Slavs. In the firſt two chapters there was frequent mention of the Goths, who seem to have practised full-timber building and ornament such as we imagine to have been used in the palace of Attila. Here we consider only the Teutons of North-weſt Europe and the British Isles.

We do not sufficiently take into account in the hiſtory of this firſt millennium the exiſtence of an indigenous tradition of timber work, not only for houses but for temples and halls (cf. my book, *Der Norden in der bildenden Kunst Westeuropas*, pp. 166 *sq*.). In England, particularly, where stonework is older than in the other parts of the Teutonic north, and where stone buildings are not only identified with the Roman occupation, there is no attempt made at a serious investigation of the influence of wood on stone architecture; merely an *a priori* argument that monuments like Earls Barton tower and Barnack can only be explained by foreign influence.[1] It will be a task of some difficulty to fix the wood technique of the various Teutonic tribes.

More important, however, for us in this book is the question: Had wood architecture in the Teutonic countries and Scandinavia—the countries in which Roman influence was not present—where no other kind of building was known, any influence on later Christian church art? It is significant that it was precisely in England, where Rome was predominant as far as the *limes*, that literary sources contain references to a *mos Scottorum* of the peoples which did come under the domination of the Roman Church.

In consequence of the geographical situation of the Continent of North-west Europe and the British Isles, they were first under the influence of the Roman Empire and Church; and later the Saracenic movement from the South, and the Norman from the North reached the frontiers. This part of Northern Europe was therefore unable to preserve its main influence undisturbed; forests had been destroyed and the old timber technique had been turned in new directions. But were the conditions always similar? It is interesting that the *mos Scottorum* was not a *mos Romanorum* or stone architecture, but the employment of an indigenous and independent northern raw material, wood. It was fortunate for Europe that the Roman power could not destroy the freedom of the entire North, and that the old cultures remained in Ireland, Scotland, and the North of Europe—cultures, and not, as ancient Romans and modern humanists see it, barbarism.

Timber work is found where certain kinds of trees were present. Half-timber work appears to have been in vogue in all countries which had an abundance of leafy trees, especially oak. The presence of wood and its use in preference to stone, which was difficult to import, particularly marble, was the surest guarantee of the free development of the art natural to

---

[1] Cf. Baldwin Brown, *op. cit.*, II., 37 ff.

these countries. The craft of wood building was natural to the men of the northern countries, as were the domestic arts to the women. Serious research is called for into the history of the forests, and especially of the oak and pine. It would show that the presence of pines leads to full timber, and the oak to half-timber building. Bede defines building *more Scottorum* as being *de robore secto*. That is, it seems, of sufficient significance for half-timber work, and we need not be surprised to find the same thing to-day. More intensive study should bring to light important facts, of which one specially strikes me. We may say, for instance, that the first step in Gothic architecture was the use by the Normans, as in the church of La Trinité at Caen, of the burying-vault or arched brace, to which Gall and Pinder trace the ribbed sexpartite vault. They have not investigated the possible origin in wood architecture of this arched brace. Pinder takes the possibility into account for the Holy Trinity Church, but does not follow the argument back to wood building in general. In my opinion, the English churches shown above (p. 82), Marton and Nether Peover, show how the arched brace originated. It is possible only with oak cut for the purpose, never with pine. That is the technical reason for its appearance. It is only in England, apparently, that there are surviving monuments to support this statement. These arched braces are not only used in half-timber churches, but are well known in stone churches about 1300 and later. Dr. Cox [1] gives a list and thirty-four illustrations, two of which I reproduce (Fig. 50 (*a*), (*b*)).

The Teutonic peoples of the Continent and the countries round the North Sea habitually built in wood, and it may be that originally all practised full-timber work. Possibly about the time of the birth of Christ a change took place, due perhaps to economic conditions, the decrease in the forest areas, and the specialization of handicrafts in these countries. Whatever may be the truth about the evolution of styles in the past, it may be observed to-day in Germany that the use of half in preference to full-timber work marks the contrast between the German peoples and the Slavs. German wooden churches, in general, are built in half-timber work : full-timber churches are (except in the mountains) the work of non-German peoples. Difference of blood seems to appear in the different styles of wooden churches ; so, for instance,

[1] *Op. cit.*, p. 273.

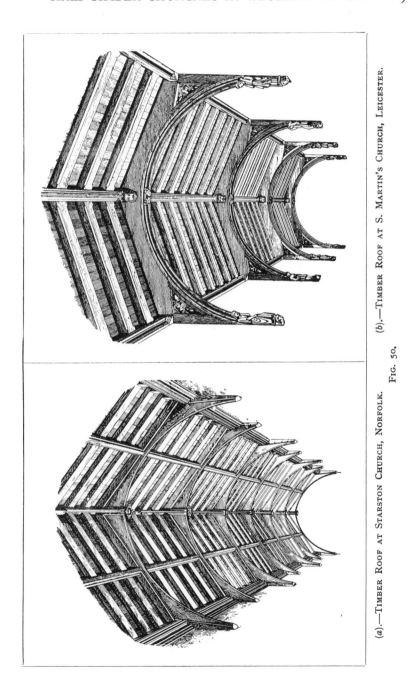

(a).—TIMBER ROOF AT STARSTON CHURCH, NORFOLK.   (b).—TIMBER ROOF AT S. MARTIN'S CHURCH, LEICESTER.

FIG. 50.

during the war of 1914-18 the Italians were building in
stone in the same region of the Alps in which the Austro-
Hungarians were constructing rectangular blockwork buildings.

This factor of blood further raises the question whether
the Celtic or the Teutonic peoples were the first to build in
half-timber work. If *mos Scottorum* signifies half-timber work,
the Celts were the forerunners. On the other hand, Fortunatus, if we have read him aright, an Italian appointed to a
Celtic bishopric admired half-timber work on the Moselle and
Rhine ; [1] that is to say, that it was not usual in Roman and
Celtic territory for houses, but was an essential feature of
Teutonic countries. We began to study these important
problems, but it is clear that they can at present only be put
as questions the time for answering which has not yet arrived.

It would not be surprising if we found from rare monuments—or, better, from documentary evidence—that the half-
timbered church type, a simple rectangular room with the
entrance on the long south side, was already the normal
pre-Christian type among Teutonic peoples. That temples
and halls were of this type is shown by the Song of Beowulf,
the Eddas, and the description of the temple at Upsala by
Saxo Grammaticus. For England the possibility that a pagan
temple was used as a Christian church is evident from a letter
of Pope Gregory the Great,[2] who expresses his desire that the
missionaries should not destroy the pagan buildings, but that,
having destroyed the idols, they should use them as churches
for divine service.

I do not think that on the Continent these Teutonic temples
commonly contained idols, nor do I think that we can explain
from them, on the same principle as that by which we can
trace the wooden church back to the wooden temple, why
statues in the early Gothic period are so frequently wooden.
The tendency to represent the human figure was not innate
in northern art ; it must rather be explained by southern influence, or by some new force such as the feeling for architecture as an organism which was the beginning of Gothic
art and which introduced plants, animals, and the human
figure into northern art.[3]

[1] Cf. my *Der Norden in der bild. Kunst Westeuropas*, pp. 103 *sq.*
[2] Bede, *Hist. Eccl.*, I., 30.
[3] Of great interest are the wooden monumental effigies in England
and Wales, collected by Mr. Fryer in his book *Wooden Monumental Effigies
in England and Wales.*

2. *The Influence of the Ruling Princes on Architecture.*— We learn from descriptions of the Heorot's hall and of the palace of Attila that timber work was used for important buildings. Neither building, however, was of half-timber work, the one being, as I would think, of the mast-type ; the other, full timber. The best example of a building whose form was dictated by a prince is the Alhambra, which has only survived by a miracle : a single spark would have meant destruction. Like the palaces of the last century in Cairo, it is built of wood and plaster. It is a proof that even in ancient times it was usual to build a palace in wood : the tradition must have come from the Indo-Iranian East. Such a palace is built by the prince not, like the mosque, for all time, but only for his own lifetime, and his successor must build one afresh. The first consideration in such buildings is a rich exterior, with gardens, and inside courts and fountains to give the appropriate character to the whole. Buildings designed for liturgical purposes have always been of a more durable material than secular buildings.

In Western Europe the use of stone in Christian times for building palaces begins with Charles the Great, the Church having been much earlier in adopting it. The second introduction of Christianity into England is an illustration of this, and we have the examples of Ripon and Hexham. Wilfrid brought from Rome the new basilica with its columns and splendid ornament : *nam in Hrypis basilicam polito lapide a fundamentis in terra usque ad summum ædificatam et porticibus suffultam in altum erexit et consumavit.*[1] And, speaking of the church of S. Andrew at Ægustaltitæ : *Cuius profunditatem in terra cum domibus mirefice politis lapidibus fundatam, et super terram multiplicem domum columnis variis et porticibus multis suffultam mirabilique longitudine et altitudine murorum ornatam . . . ullam domum aliam citra Alpes montes talem aedificatam audivimus . . . magnalia ornamenta huius multiplicis domus de auro et argento lapidibusque, pretiosis et quomodo altaria purpura et serico induta decoravit.*[2] In this way, about the end of the seventh century the Roman church introduced the new representative style, and, unhappily, from the point of view of northern art, brought to an end the old northern tradition of wood architecture.

---

[1] *Vita Wilfredi*, XVII.
[2] *Ibid.*, XXI., Acta SS. Ord. S. Benedicti Sc., IV., 1, 688.

We can therefore say with certainty that quarry-stone building was brought to the North of Europe from the Mediterranean. After the Roman period it was the Christian emperor, the king, the bishop, and other temporal and spiritual powers that introduced it. Later on, monasteries played their part in its evolution. In no other part of Northern Europe was the change from wood to stone so absolute as in the western part, which accordingly showed the way to the whole of Europe ; the true bearers of the new southern stone architecture were monasteries and, especially in the beginning, the Benedictines.

3. *Spread of New Styles.*—We saw that the type of half-timber work which we met with in church architecture in Western Europe and the British Isles could be a European creation, but could also originate in the southern countries, where wood had become rare at a far earlier period. Those parts of Ireland and Scotland which were not completely under the Roman domination retained the old types of wood and stone building. Another starting-point for the study of half-timber work may be found in the poems of Venantius Fortunatus, which point perhaps to the use in the Rhenish towns of a kind of timber work. Other literary sources and monuments attest the prevalence of timber churches.

An important fact is that the Scottish monks, coming to the Continent as missionaries, who had been accustomed to build their churches *more Scottorum*, that is to say, *de robore secto*, and *tabulis dedolatis*, found that this technique was identical with that of the Teutonic peoples. The opposite was the case centuries later when the lands which to-day show the widest area of half-timber churches—Brandenburg, Mecklenburg, and Pomerania—were newly colonized by German peoples. They brought the Teutonic type to countries which for centuries had been occupied by Slavs, and where full-timber work had been general. It seems safe to say that in the first thousand years of our era all the West European peoples used half-timber, a tradition which was destroyed only by the Roman Church in England from about 600, and on the Continent from about 1050.

Again the question arises—At what time and with which peoples did half-timber work reach the North of Europe ? Did it begin with the Celts, afterwards reaching the Germans, and did it perhaps eventually at some time later also reach the Slavs ? It seems possible that the East Germans,

PLATE XXXVII

(*a* and *b*) Panels of the Franks Casket (British Museum)

(*c*) Modern Restoration of an Old English Half-Timber Church

PLATE XXXVIII

(b) Greenstead Church : the Old Beams

(a) Greenstead, Essex : Old Material in a New Church

who migrated from their country, learnt in the East to build in full timber.

In considering the movement of wood architecture to the southern peninsulas, the influence of the Lombards is of particular interest. We saw that the Croatians, moving, as the Goths had done earlier to Spain from East to West, brought full-timber work and vaulting to the Balkans. It is quite otherwise in Italy, when in 568, after a short sojourn in Hungary, the Lombards moved thence from the Teutonic North. There they used neither the vault nor the square plan, but adopted the type of the early Christian basilica. This would be difficult to explain if the Lombards had not come from a northern country where rectangular buildings with raftered roofs were general. This type, and the Norwegian, with twelve masts, so nearly resemble the Hellenistic or Roman basilica that it is not hard to conceive of the Lombards building their churches with three aisles like the Roman basilica instead of one-aisled, both kinds having raftered roofs.

Now are we to believe that the flourishing period of the half-timber church in the second half of the first thousand years of our era had no influence on the later West European stone architecture? This national and original wooden church architecture was followed by the great styles of stonework which are called Romanesque and Gothic. Is it credible that the old tradition of the wood builder did not leave its mark on the development of both of the new styles, and is there not, on the face of it, an urgent need for research on this chapter of art and history to rescue it from the neglect of scholars?

The most important point remaining to be settled, which links up the present subject with our investigations in Armenia and Dalmatia, is whether this West European half-timber architecture, like the full-timber work in the East, had not some essential motive which separates the Roman from the Romanesque church. In Carolingian times, as we noticed in Croatia, churches were built of a square type vaulted by a cupola which had its origin in full-timber work. In West European mediæval architecture there is one feature which may be said to have a parallel in half-timber church building, namely, successions of arches and frames (*Gurt und Joch*) in a long series. This architectural conception seems to be the most salient feature of that kind of church building, which, compared with all the styles known to the world at the time, is most typical of the West European styles that we call

Romanesque and Gothic. In Syria we find a type of church built in the basalt stone of the Hauran in this manner, but there, by reason of its Arabian or wooden origin, a broad church is demanded, changed only by Hellenistic influence into a long church. We see, too, in Roman architecture, bath-buildings with three parts in this style; but only in Western Europe, as the last stage in the evolutionary process, do we find the long church with arches and frames in a continuous succession.

The half-timber churches illustrated in this chapter consistently show this scheme. Is it here that we must look for the origin of a similar arrangement in northern stone architecture?

If, as we have supposed, there was a flourishing wood architecture both of half-timber and full-timber work in the north of the continent of Europe, with the introduction of stone as the chief building material builders must have been faced with the problem of how the popular wooden technique could be translated into stone, or rather how the new southern stone building could be regarded from the standpoint of the carpenter and his methods. The new basilican type was transmitted by monks, but it was only at the beginning that the ordinary builder came from the South. As time went on the influence of the geographical situation, the country and the national temperament began to adapt the Roman forms to their own ideas, with the result that the new system of arches and frames came in, which was the fundamental principle of the two great styles of the Middle Ages.

One of the chief features of half-timber architecture which later weighed much with builders in stone in the North, and which is to be attributed entirely to the northern influences, is the undivided nave which is characteristic of the half-timber church, divisions into two parts being exceptional, and into three, due often to the influence of the southern basilica. Thus we observe a certain conflict between the preferences for the nave in three parts and for undivided rooms, the latter being favoured by the North, while the former was a foreign style. The hall-church may have been the first stage, the solution being found only in the Baroque period, and by means of the cupola, an early northern type (cf. my *Armenia*).

I am not convinced that the vault has an independent origin in half-timber work. The more must I insist that vaulting is an early creation of full-timber architecture (p. 54).

Here we may merely refer to the possibilities in cases where full-timber building is combined with raftered roofs, which are the characteristic feature of half-timber work.

Reverting to what was said at the opening of the chapter, we may remark that in Germany, France, and still more in England, the field lies open for research. The rare examples of half-timber churches are not inevitably imitations of stone buildings ; they are rather the remains of a flourishing wood architecture in pagan and early Christian times, which exercised a strong influence on the later stone churches of the Anglo-Saxons and Normans, and the great styles which we call Romanesque and Gothic. At one time the carpenter was the real and the only architect in the North. In Germany it was not till about 1050 that for Christian church architecture the best of these builders gravitated to the stone-cutter's yard, where greater ability was called for and higher wages were paid.

It is to be hoped that this chapter may do something to discourage the unintelligent restoration of old timber churches with which we are too familiar. Serious work is out of the question in these circumstances. Plate XXXVII. (*c*) is a conspicuous instance, and we may recall the treatment of the monuments at Aix-la-Chapelle [1] and on the Rhine by the ex-Kaiser.

[1] Strzygowski, *Der Dom zu Aachen und seine Entstellung.*

CHAPTER IV.

THE MAST-CHURCHES OF NORWAY.

WE now see that there are two different types of wood architecture in continental Europe—full-timber blockwork in the
East and half-timber in the West. In this chapter I point to
a third European type, of which Norway alone has preserved
examples, and which I call " mast-churches." They are of
particular interest to English people, since it is said that
Norway received them as she received Christianity—from the
British Isles—where, indeed, there was a type of wood
architecture known as *mos Scottorum*, which I dealt with in
the third chapter and in my chapter on Hiberno-Saxon church
art (*Origin of Christian Church Art*, Oxford, 1923). At Greenstead, Essex, can be seen the remains of " the oldest wooden
church " in England, a very simple type with walls in so-called
stave-work. But it is not the modern church that interests us.
It is rather the long row of ancient timbers placed vertically
side by side on both walls and at the west end with the wooden
tower. Plate XXXVIII. (*a*) shows a general view of the
walls, and Plate XXXVIII. (*b*) gives the detail of how the
timbers are placed.[1] Formerly they were fastened at both
ends to sleepers, or horizontal timbers : to-day they rest on
horizontal beams cut in accordance with the modern foundation, but at the top it can be seen how they were originally
fixed. In Plate XXXVIII. (*b*) it will be noticed how part of
each timber is cut away so that it may fit into the sleeper.
This is the type known as the stave-wall or " stave-church."
In the present chapter, however, we are only concerned with
another type in which walls of this kind are found, the richly
decorated Norwegian churches, to which I give the name of
" mast-churches."

In dealing with the east and west of Europe we had to
reconstruct mentally the older types from later fairly well-
preserved monuments. In Norway a more direct method is
possible, since the monuments preserved do not belong to

---

[1] Both photographs taken by Mr. Arthur Gardner.

recent centuries, but go back to a time much nearer to that in which we are interested, namely, the early North European or pre-Romanesque period. It is for this reason that the monuments are of such value : we can base our investigations not on the types, but on the monuments themselves. Very few of those early wooden churches remain : each one, though it cannot be placed in a museum, is a museum in itself. There are, it may be noted, several churches in the open-air museums of Scandinavia. First of all I shall describe one or two of the churches, and later I shall discuss the essential character and the evolution of the types.

At this point I am tempted to inquire whether this important group is known to students. The question is, perhaps, indiscreet, but I know from experience that little interest is taken in these wooden churches. I shall have succeeded in my object if I have aroused some interest in buildings which are the only monuments next to the period for which I am claiming attention. We are excavating in all directions in the southern area. If scientific work is more than a passing fashion, surely we must realize that it is our duty to excavate in the North also. For the moment we need not dig with the spade, but we can surely unearth the books which, though published a good many years ago, have lain neglected.

I. **Study of the Monuments.**—In 1837 Dahl drew attention to the mast-churches in a book, written in German, *Monuments of a very Early Century in the Inner Regions of Norway*. Some years later a society was formed for the preservation of Norwegian antiquities, and in 1854, under its auspices, was published Nicolaysen's book on the monuments of mediæval art. It is to this society that we owe the preservation of the most valuable examples of mediæval wooden churches in Europe. One of the earliest, the church at Urnes, possibly of the eleventh or twelfth century, attests the height to which wooden architecture rose before the Roman Church and the monks made an end of the old wood tradition. From 1050 the stone church begins to supersede the wooden church in the North.

The Norwegian mast-churches have been better known since the publication by L. Dietrichson of his book, *De Norske Stavkirker*. A second edition, in German, *Die Holzbauten Norwegens in Vergangenheit und Gegenwart*, appeared in 1893. In the first place, I must again draw attention to the fact that they date from the Middle Ages. I wonder if it is realized that in this humid northern region we possess entire buildings of wood from the eleventh or twelfth century to the Reformation. In no other country, not excepting the British Isles, is there any wooden monument of so early a date. S. Andrew's Church, Greenstead, is so much restored that it is difficult to argue from this single exception. In Norway there is evidence of 322 churches of the Middle Ages—that is to say, of the kind we call mediæval or mast-churches. In 1893 Dietrichson counted twenty-four still standing.

I select two churches for detailed description, the churches at Borgund and Urnes—the one as being the finest example from the point of view of architecture, the other as having the richest ornament.

S. Andrew's Church at Borgund lies to the north-east of Bergen at the end of the Sognfjord, on the way to Oslo. It belongs to the society for the preservation of Norwegian antiquities, by whom it was restored. The church is first mentioned in a document of 1360, but the style of the inscriptions and ornaments points to 1150. This corresponds to the Norman period in English architecture, at which, following the building of Winchester Cathedral (1079-97) and Norwich (from 1096), the great cathedrals of Ely (1102-74) and Peterborough (1170-93) were built, the influence of which is seen in Norway, in Stavanger (c. 1123-50), and the first stone cathedral of Drontheim. At the same time, the old wooden architecture in Norway was still in a perfect state.

Plate XXXIX. (a) [1] shows the church in its natural surroundings. It is built in a rocky valley between high mountains, and its height, 49½ feet, is one of its most striking artistic values : in this connection it is interesting to note that it is in six stages. It will be at once observed that the roofs are orientated from west to east, as we have seen in some of the churches of Eastern Europe of a later date. There is also, however, a vertical line marked by the small spire and, lower, by gables on the roofs. The small round tower at the east and the dragons' heads on the roofs should also be noticed. In the foreground of Plate XXXIX. (a) may be seen a wooden steeple. Fig. 51 gives the plan of the church. The ground plan is a square, 23½ × 19½ feet. To understand the construction, we must begin not with the floor itself, but with

[1] I have to thank Mr. Martin Olsson for the photographs of Norwegian churches which I reproduce here.

PLATE XXXIX

(*a*) Borgund, Norway : The Steeple and Church

(*b*) Borgund Church : Detail of Interior

PLATE XL

(b) Urnes Church, Norway : Detail of Interior

(a) Borgund Church : Detail of Interior

four sleepers under the floor, laid so as to enclose a square, the ends crossing at the corners and projecting beyond the walls. At each of the points of intersection (15½ × 11½ feet) stands a mast, and there are two on each side of this mast (each 25½ feet high)—twelve in all. As the church is not an exact square, the distance between the two masts on the longer sides is greater than that between the masts on the shorter sides. A thirteenth and a fourteenth mast might be expected on the long sides, but they are not present. This fact is important, and it must also be noticed particularly that the entrance and the apse are blocked by two masts.

The twelve masts do not themselves give the ground plan of the church. Parallel to the rows of masts and 3 feet distant there are thin walls or, more correctly, screens, from which these churches have been given what I think a misleading name, "stave-churches," whereas it is the sleepers and masts which are the essential and fundamental elements of the structure. The walls are mere boundaries and auxiliary to the

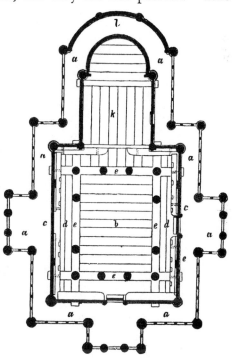

FIG. 51.—PLAN OF BORGUND CHURCH, NORWAY.

masts, which support the roof. The " walls " are a species of framework : in each corner is a round pillar connected with its neighbours by two beams, the lower lying on the sleepers, the upper resting on the corner pillars. Each wall is built up of vertical boards, or, more properly, beams cut in half, as we have seen in the case of Greenstead.

Fig. 52 gives a section showing how the masts are vertically fixed by connecting boards cut in the form of horse-shoe arches with two continuous horizontal timbers between which the pillars are connected by intersecting diagonals. Immediately above there are horse-shoe arches again (Fig. 52). At the top the masts are all connected by beams and anchors, the whole supporting the main gabled roof which is 35½ feet in height, im- mediately below which are very small round windows. Then comes the second part of the roof over the aisles, supported by the masts.

The interior of the church has at

FIG. 52.—SECTION OF BORGUND CHURCH.

the east end the rectangular choir, 11 feet square, which in Borgund terminates in a semi-circular apse of later date.

Round the entire church runs a broad embowered walk with pillars and arcade outside, 5 feet 2 inches in height, which forms in the bays small vestibules, the roofs of which are seen in Plate XXXIX. (*b*).

FIG. 53.—BORGUND CHURCH. DETAIL OF MAST CONSTRUCTION.

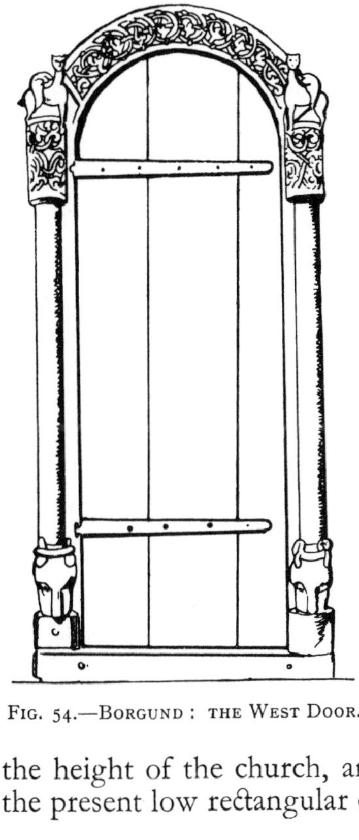

There is no rich decoration in the Borgund church. The interior is plain timber work. Plate XL. (*a*) shows the lower part of the masts ; only the connecting diagonals are decorated, having foliate ornament outside and ribs inside. Beyond the side arcades are human heads, which are also found at the ends of the masts at the junction with the roof (Plate XXXIX. (*b*)). Outside, at the west end, there is a richly carved door with an arch and dragons ; but the only early part seems to me to be the simpler west door (Fig. 54), with interlaced work on the arch and the capitals of two masts with animal heads on the lower part and scrolls on the top.

The church at Urnes, north of Borgund, at the end of the Sognfjord, shows traces of a very rich ornamentation. The date first assigned to it was 1323, but it is said to have been built about 1100, and to be the oldest extant wooden church of Norway. It is, of course, not the oldest church, as there are among the later types many much earlier forms. Plate XLI. (*a*) shows the exterior from the north-east. Three parts of the church may be seen, the main part with a small belfry on the roof, a prolongation of the church in length, almost equal to the height of the church, and the addition at the east end of the present low rectangular choir. In the background are the

FIG. 54.—BORGUND : THE WEST DOOR.

fjord and some houses. We are concerned only with the

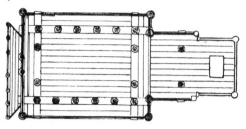

main body of the church. It will be remembered that in the plan of the church of Borgund (Fig. 51) there were two pairs of sleepers, and at each angle three masts : the church at Urnes (Fig.

FIG. 55.—PLAN OF THE CHURCH AT URNES, NORWAY.

55), however, is relatively much longer (28 × 21½ feet), and there are six columns in a row, each 15 feet from its neighbour, in the nave, and 3¼ feet from the stave-walls. Looking at the interior (Plate XLII. (a)) we find at the east end of the square plan a column in the middle. This column, however, is thinner than the others and, like that on its left, is to-day cut off at the top of the screen.

The north-east corner of the interior is illustrated in Plate XLI. (b). Instead of masts reaching to the roof as at Borgund, we find genuine columns with cube-capitals. Above are independent masts separated by boards and stout beams. These angular masts (Plate XL. (b)) are ornamented with scrolls and extend to the roof. The upper part between them is closed by three boards with a small round window in the middle. The roof is 34 feet high, the walls 22½ feet.

Round the outside of the church ran a cloistered path 3½ feet wide, as at Borgund, but to-day there remains only a small part in front of the west entrance, the rest having been removed in 1772.

Better known than the church building is the ornament, which is the finest remaining to us of the early mediæval period in Norway. At the north-east end, by the wall, is a decorated round corner column with a cubical base (Fig. 56), a remark-

FIG. 56.—URNES: DETAIL OF CARVED BASE OF COLUMN.

able feature. We shall see later that cube capitals and bases have been said to be copied from Romanesque stonework. Then we come to the next corner and nine

PLATE XLI

(a) Urnes Church, Norway: General View

(b) Urnes Church: Detail of Interior at North-East corner

PLATE XLII

(b) Fortun Church, Norway : Detail of Roof

(a) Urnes Church : The Interior

undecorated panels: of the panels that follow, the tenth and twelfth, like the adjacent door, are richly decorated (Plate XLIV. (*a*)). Recalling the Croatian or Lombard stone decoration, we realize their crudity in comparison with this fine woodwork. Here we have a northern original of the pre-Romanesque period. When we look at work of such a character coming from a simple church carpenter, we are prepared for the royal tomb of earlier date, which we shall see in the last chapter. It is the earliest of the wooden monuments that are of the highest quality.

While we do not find the geometrical interlaced bands, the interlaced ornament with animals arises from the same feeling for the moving line; instead of circles and intersecting lines there are dismembered animals rendered with great freedom and richness of interlacing. The board which forms the horse-shoe arch on the door has fine lines spread over the surface. The contrast to the neighbouring boards, carved in higher relief, is very striking, particularly the lines crossing the top of the horse-shoe festoon-wise outside the field of the ornament.

FIG. 57.—URNES: ORNAMENT ON THE WEST GABLE.

The west gable (Fig. 57) has the same ornament spread over the vertical boards: it represents a standing animal being bitten in the neck by another animal, perhaps a serpent. This central motive is interlaced with fine lines.

What does art-history say of these two buildings at Borgund and Urnes? Dietrichson has given precedence to them in his book (p. 74), and his example is followed by every book in which they are mentioned. The stave-church, he says, is an ingenious translation of the stone church into wood, and he adduces as his most conclusive proof the older church at Urnes. It is more on the model of the three-aisled stone basilica, he thinks, than the later churches where wood architecture has come into its own. In the columns with cube-capitals, in the upper masts which he calls " lisenes," in the details of the arches, and in the figures on the capitals, he sees the characteristic forms of Romanesque stone architecture. But is that correct?

II. Essential Character of Mast-church Art.—It is important that we should arrive at a clear conception of the type which has been erroneously called the stave-church. Arbitrary solutions to problems of this kind, especially those which are not on the lines of the time-honoured principles of æsthetic, may lead to a total misunderstanding of the valuable material available in Norway.

1. *Raw Material and Technique.*—What do we mean when we speak of a mast-church ? In the last chapters we studied the wooden churches of the last few centuries in the East and West of Europe. We saw that there was a very large number of wooden churches of late date, but of quite a different type of workmanship. Instead of the early mast-churches of Norway we have there, in the West, framework ; in the East, blockwork churches, depending upon the amount of wood available, with the intermediate blockwork churches with raftered—that is to say, framework—roof. With these the mast-church has no connection.

Is it conceivable that a type like the early Christian basilica, or even the Norman or Romanesque basilicas, could have even been the prototype of the eleventh or twelfth century Norwegian wooden churches ? From purely technical reasons this seems to me impossible. In the stone basilicas there are solid walls and two long rows of columns of about the same height as the walls. Why should the builder use sleepers rather than well-bonded walls ? Clearly sleepers and masts are the germ of the idea. If we consider two sleepers crossing one another, then in the place of crossing we see the natural place to fix one mast : two pairs give four crossing-points for masts. But this would not be the first step if the builder had in view two rows of columns, and still less if he contemplated building walls ; in a stave-church, the name notwithstanding, the walls are not an integral part of the structure.

Returning to the plan of the Borgund church (Fig. 51), we are met by the remarkable fact that instead of two rows of columns, the four masts in the corners, each with an additional mast on either side, are the essential feature of the construction. These corner-masts are also found at Urnes (Fig. 55). In this way, however, the entrance and the chancel are blocked by two or more columns, for which a parallel may possibly be found in early Jewish synagogues in Palestine, but never in an ordinary Christian basilica. This is entirely contrary to the principles by which a basilica is constructed, and no builder desiring to reproduce a stone basilica in wood would ever work on such a plan.

Had there been any desire to translate the Roman stone basilica into wood the natural technique would have been blockwork or framework, certainly not the exceptional combination of sleepers and beams. A comparison of these techniques one with another will at once illustrate the point. There could hardly be a greater contrast than that of the block church of Eastern Europe, in which the roof is supported by four walls, with the churches of the north-west of Europe in which sleepers and masts sustain the roof of an interior with stave screens resting on the ends of sleepers. In the former a heavy mass of level wood is the outer covering, unsupported by interior scaffolding, while the latter is primarily a structure of standing beams and masts, the interior covered with a surface of boards. In West European framework a repetition of the frame gives a row of rectangular sections with an outer covering, which may be one of several kinds of material. This, however, never takes the form of sleepers and masts.

It can hardly be doubted that the building of the mediæval churches in Norway shows a finished technique, which can only be explained on the hypothesis of a high level of craftsmanship already in existence. The blockwork and framework techniques point to a plentiful or a scanty supply of wood; the stave-church, however, is of its kind a masterpiece, and possesses an individuality of its own. It does not imitate a foreign church type—we have seen possible translations into blockwork in the wooden basilicas of Slovakia—but it is an individual creation independent of Rome or Byzantium, as are the stone churches of Armenia, Dalmatia, Visigothic Spain, and the West and South Slavonic square churches. All are related to the early wood architecture. Old framework churches of the west have not survived; the block churches of the Middle Ages are also destroyed: the mast-churches of Norway alone are left to us in their original form: they show the independence of the wood architect's craft at that time. It will be remembered that we attempted to reconstruct it when we were dealing with Slavonic architecture, working back from the later examples. The description of the church at Borgund illustrates the technique: sleepers holding the roof-masts at the points of intersection and supporting the screen or wall of staves at their extremities. The most interesting feature is the ingenious manner in which the parts reaching upwards are connected. We may compare in this connection the clay and wood buildings found by Sir Aurel Stein in the Khotan. There the roof was vaulted with unburnt bricks. In Norway the construction is entirely of wood. The roof, as may be seen (Plate XLII. (*b*)) in the church of Fortun (now in Fantoft near Bergen), is divided into sections by arches in the framework which continue the masts. These last reach to the roof, as described above, and, as at Borgund, are connected in various ways ; at the top, between the roof of the side-aisles and the sloping roof of the building, we see the small round windows (Plate XL. (*b*)). If this is not sufficiently clear, the open rafters will be recognized, between which on each side of the roof are inverted arches. The scheme is more clearly seen in the interior of the small church of Torpe, in Hallingdal (Plate XLIII. (*b*)). The building between the masts is different here as in Urnes (Plate XL. (*b*)) or Borgund (Plate XXXIX. (*b*)), resembling that at Fortun (Plate XLII. (*b*)). First, as at the last-mentioned place, we have boards cut into a semi-circle between the cube-capitals, then the first beam which meets the mast at the angle, next come the intersecting diagonals. There is, however, no second horizontal beam, and we go on to the second semi-circular arch. These parts should be remembered, as we shall return to them later in connection with the catch-phrase " triforium." Behind the lower arches and the capitals may be seen the inverted arches in the roofs of the side-aisles, and the same arches will be recognized in the main roof.

It is the occurrence of the inverted arches that has led the experts in treating this remarkable roofing technique to the conclusion that this open roof has no connection with the timbered roof of the Roman basilica, but, on the contrary, directly suggests the technique of shipbuilding, having the appearance of an inverted boat. Seesselberg illustrated this resemblance in drawings (Plate XLV. (*b*) and Fig. 65). For the moment I cannot pursue this subject further, but we shall return to it in the last chapter. It is, moreover, unnecessary, since experts are agreed that the problem of building wooden churches in this manner was solved by a people versed in the technique of shipbuilding, as certain technical details prove. It seems, therefore, at least possible that this church type was derived from shipbuilding. The art-historian, however, disagrees : these wooden churches, he says, are copies of earlier stone churches, which by degrees acquired the forms characteristic of wood buildings. In tracing wooden churches to shipbuilding, therefore, we put forward a theory which he considers idle and fantastic.

The magnitude of the mast-church builder's achievement is fully realized only by those who are acquainted with the other types of wooden churches in Europe, blockwork and framework ; and more than these, it presupposes an already highly developed technique, which we find in shipbuilding.

Ornament.—The same artistic feeling appears in the decoration. The finest block-churches are sparingly decorated, the corners, doors, and window showing modest ornament ; in framework-churches the contrast of the frame and the means by which it is filled in is emphasized : the mast-church had richly decorated furniture, like that which we found copied from stone in Croatian church art. In the last lecture we shall see some wooden originals. The mast-churches dating, like that of Urnes, from about 1100, have furniture of comparatively late date ; the altar chancel and other objects belong to the last few centuries (Plate XLII. (*a*)), not, like the churches themselves, to mediæval times. It is to be regretted that in the north there is no church furniture contemporary with the Lombardian or Croatian stone copies which we found in the southern peninsulas. We

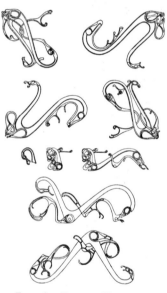

Fig. 58.—Typical Northern "Animal" Ornament.

must deduce the probable technique of the furniture from the churches themselves : at Urnes we saw that the walls and, still more, the doors are finely ornamented in low relief.

There is a wide difference between the Norwegian and the Croatian ornament. The ornament on the stone before 1100 is geometrical, that of the wooden churches after 1100 is the well-known animal ornament (Plate XLIV. (*b*) and Fig. 58). The contrast is increased when we consider the added artistic value of the shape. Comparing the doorways of Croatian (Plate XLV. (*c*)) and Norwegian churches (Fig. 59), we find in the former, stones laid vertically and horizontally ; in the latter, two vertical side planks with two masts and two small boards, the one including the arch itself, the other filling the spandrels within the rectangular (п-shaped) frame ; the Norwegian technique is true stave-work, just as the Croatian is true block (or, later, stone) work.

2. *Significance.* —It may be asked whether the fact that the building was to be used as a church in any way influenced the architectural type wrongly called "stave-church." I think not. It seems quite probable that before the Vikings applied the ingenious combination of sleepers, masts, stave-work, and the shipbuilding technique for churches, they had already used it in pagan times for secular buildings. There is a type of monument, well known from documentary evidence (not, it

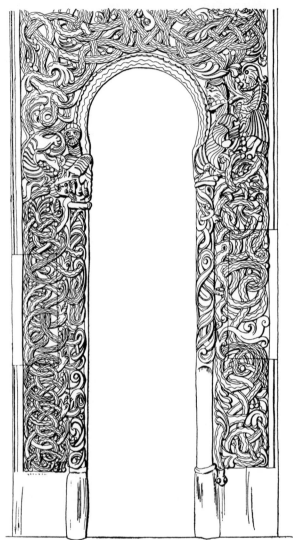

FIG. 59.—TYPICAL DOORWAY TO NORWEGIAN MAST-CHURCH.

may be remarked, written in Latin), and described as having been the centre of social life at the time, namely, the hall. The best-known is King Hrothgar's hall, described at length and in some detail in the romance of Beowulf. This Anglo-

Saxon poem is earlier than any of the Scandinavian Christian churches : it is the *locus classicus* for the wood architecture of the countries on the North Sea, as is the account of Attila's palace given by Priskos for blockwork, and the poem of Prudentius for Rhenish framework. Hrothgar's hall is the type which later becomes the mast or stave-church : the pagan richness of ornament is suggested in the account of the coloured vermiculated ornament on the high walls of the building. Another similar hall we find in Snorres Heimskringla (about 1230), the most famous wood building in Norway, built by King Sigurd (1103-30).

The second example of the mast-church type is the wooden pagan temple. Adam of Bremen (about 1070) makes some observations on the ancient temple of Upsala, which he terms a triclinium with the statue of Tor and two others in the centre.[1] This, too, we may reconstruct in the form of a hall of stave-church with masts round the wall and the sloping roof bearing upon the centre. In the Eddas we found other literary evidences of wooden temples. In Iceland excavations revealed only some primitive stone rectangular buildings with a separate compartment on one of the shorter sides.

Ornament.—Is it conceivable that the ornament which we have seen at Urnes, and shall find in other mast-churches, was derived from the spirit of the church ? That is not the case. In ornament, as in architecture, the church had recourse to a pagan type. In the next chapter we shall see animal ornament, and particularly in conjunction with the geometrical pattern which we met with on the Croatian monuments. In the north, as we shall find, not only metal-work, but ships, house-furniture, cars, sledges, and other objects of astonishing richness, all belonging to pagan times, were decorated. Their significance, therefore, cannot be particularly Christian, but must belong to pre-Christian times. Animal ornament is peculiarly appropriate to the arts which bear upon ordinary life, such as the building of ships or houses. I have several times in my books had occasion to allude to the Iranian " Hvarenah," in which the glory of God is symbolized by animals, plants, or the landscape itself.[2] The theory suggests itself of a religious stream starting from Iran and running along the old Indo-Aryan migration routes to the European world,

[1] Another temple is mentioned in the Saga of the Golden Gnorri.
[2] *Origin of Christian Church Art*, pp. 118 *sq.*

bringing the animal ornament to the north when in the Hellenistic Roman and early Christian periods it was entering the Mediterranean countries. We shall revert to this when we come to investigate the source of the animal forms which transformed the previous geometrical ornaments.

3. *Shape.*—The essential difference between the hall and the church before about 1000 is that, while the hall has its main entrance on the long south side immediately opposite the chair of the owner, in the church the entrance is later on the short west side, or on one or both of the long sides, the altar being always at the short east end. Thus the hall is broad, the church long. The point which is to be noted here is that from the general type either a hall or a church can be evolved. What, then, is the general type?

We showed that owing to its architectural technique the Norwegian church could not be an imitation of the Roman basilica, but had as its fundamental element two pairs of sleepers, with four masts at the points of crossing. It would clearly add weight to our theory if we could point to mast-churches with four masts only. These exist, and are found principally in the diocese of Stavanger. Dietrichson describes them as " the Valdres type with four columns." Plate XLV (*a*) shows the church of Lomen. In his drawing of this church it is to be feared that Dietrichson shows a complete misunderstanding of the problem : he draws four columns, and outside four others, in which are fixed the stave-work screens, but altogether leaves out the sleepers, an omission which is inconceivable on the part of one who understood the essential character of the architectural scheme. The sleepers must be drawn, if only to show the projections under the stave-screens where the masts rest on the points of intersection. Dietrichson ignores this feature : perhaps only thus could he enunciate his humanistic theory of the evolution of this type, which he states in these words :—

> " The stave-church with numerous masts is an immediate imitation of the stone basilica, but without the long rows of columns : the four-masted church, however, is built on the assumption that wood, with its greater elasticity, can dispense with the numerous supporting columns and boldly supports a single arch from mast to mast over the entire nave laterally and longitudinally. But in the triforium and the upper wall of the Valdres

church (with four masts) we clearly see the support given by columns and masts ; in three parts, therefore, staves are found, as in the Sogntype, with numerous masts."

A careful examination of these words shows that in Dietrichson's view the northern carpenter realizes only by degrees the possibilities of wood.   To me the opposite appears to be the case.   The four-mast church is the beginning ; the churches with four masts showing the earlier, those with twelve masts the later type of a larger church ; those with numerous masts showing the influence of the stone churches with two rows of columns on the older wooden type.   Borgund (Fig. 51), with its system of $4 \times 3 = 12$ masts, is a pure northern type. Urnes (Fig. 55), although the most ancient extant monument, cannot be the oldest type of mast-church : its type is, on the contrary, not pure ; a comparison with the Borgund church will show that there the Roman type disturbs the earlier tradition which must therefore be before 1100, the twelve-mast system with its two masts on each side of the corner mast gives only the superficial effect of two continuous rows of " columns."   In the main body of the church at Urnes the space between the two side-masts is open, although Plate XLII. (a) shows a central thin mast with its lower portion cut away.

If we could enter into the numerous points which at once present themselves, and if my point of view were accepted as a matter of course, we should look on art-history from the northern angle, not setting great store by the evolutionary theories of the old text-books.   I touch upon two points, the triforium and the cube-capital.   We called the system by which the masts are fixed the triforium, the name of its counterpart in Romanesque stone architecture ; and, as may be imagined, the scholars confidently assert that the Norwegian mast-churches are imitating the plan of the stone church.   We can, however, form our own opinion on the point and judge of the more probable origin of the structure.   The cube capital, as I showed in my *Armenia*, was the typical capital in Armenian churches as early as the seventh century.   It is very familiar from the mediæval churches of Britain, and still more from those of Western Germany.   Seeing them now in Norwegian wood architecture, we are led to inquire whether instead of being copies of stone originals, they are not rather the original forms like the earlier examples found so frequently in Armenia, but translated into stone as in the west and north of Europe. I do not go so far as to say that they are derived from the wood architecture of the North Sea countries, but certainly they have their origin in wood building. We are still ignorant of the plan of the early Western European framework, and the first two chapters showed that we knew but little of eastern blockwork.

FIG. 60.—TYPICAL DOOR DECORATION TO A NORWEGIAN MAST-CHURCH.

Ornament. — The discussion of these architectural details brings us to the consideration of the ornament. Most important from this point of view are the doors in the mast - churches, the structure of which has already been treated. The decoration of the two boards at the sides (Fig. 60) consists of scrolls issuing from the head of an animal to be seen near the base of the mast. The mast or column and the arch have interlaced bands or scroll ornament. In front of the arch on the capitals have been cut lions in the round, and

the corners of the ⊓-shaped frames over the arch are filled
with dragons with their extremities interlaced with one another and the tendrils on the boards. The motive of the
mast-church ornament is thus the combination of the animal
figure with the earlier interlaced band ornament round an
arcade.

In England animal ornament is well known in Anglo-Saxon
times. What is its origin? It appears on the Kremsmünster
chalice (777), and about a hundred years earlier in the Lindisfarne Gospels. Salin, in his standard work on this early
Teutonic animal ornament, states that it proceeds by three
stages and in three styles to the north of Europe. We are
therefore led to see in it the result of a general movement
northwards. I agree for the most part with Salin, and on one
point alone am I in opposition to him, and that is the humanistic bias, which has been an obsession with all who have
hitherto dealt with this subject. The animal figure, we are
told, must have come to the north of Europe as a derivative
of certain Roman motives. But can we recall any Greek or
Roman motive which has any striking affinity with the northern
animal ornament in the three styles mentioned above (Plate
XLIV. (*b*) and Fig. 58)? I do not think one could be found,
except, perhaps, some example of Eastern Hellenistic art
derived from Iran, the Asiatic outpost of the entire northern
area. We must, therefore, put away our humanistic blinkers
and refuse to be convinced by far-fetched arguments of this
kind. In works such as Minns's *Scythians and Greeks*, Rostovtzeff's *Iranians and Greeks*, and in earlier works of Finnish
or Russian scholars, a very curious fact is noted, namely, that
while the north of Europe used only the geometrical band
ornament, so northern Asia used only the animal motive. It
was never a direct copy from nature, but received a fine geometrical treatment, as is seen in the north of Europe and in
the liturgical vases of China. The animal (Plate XLIV. (*c*))
is not viewed with southern eyes—that is to say, naturalistically—and at times it cannot be specified, the only distinction
possible being between a beast and a bird. Now the types
discovered by Salin, and set forth in his *magnum opus*, are just
those the presence of which can be proved in the north, and
which in course of time came by way of Perm and the Baltic
bridge to the north of Europe. This point, however, is not
an essential one for the purpose of these chapters and I shall
not insist upon it: I have discussed it in an article entitled

" The Northern Stream of Art from Ireland to China and the Southern Movement," written for the new *Year Book of Oriental Art* (I., London, 1925).[1]   It is sufficient to say that if we can trace a movement in the North itself, and between Asia and Europe, we shall more readily assent to the theory propounded in considering the significance of this ornament. The mind of the humanistic scholar, however, refuses to admit the possibility of Iranian influences.   Animal ornament, in his opinion, must have come from the South, and the animal figure is probably taken from exported Roman ware.

Thus, too, Dietrichson considers that the combination of entire animal figures, as we have seen them on the doors, is an importation from the South or West: the North originates nothing in Europe or Asia.   But if we consider a stave-door like that shown in Figs. 59 and 60, surely we shall see that the composition is essentially oriental.   The ∩-shaped frame which I mentioned in my *Armenia*, the lions, and, in particular, the dragons, are to be found in precisely the same position over the arch in Mohammedan and Chinese art.

. 4. *Form.*—The principal artistic value of a mast-church is the height.   The essential feature is not, as in the Roman basilica, the longitudinal axis from West to East, but the perpendicular axis of the central portion, a fact which again invalidates the theory of a derivation from the basilica.   The exterior of such mast-churches as Borgund (Plate XXXIX. (*a*)), Torpe (Plate XLIII. (*a*)) built about 1200, and first mentioned in 1310, or the contemporary church of Gol (Plate XLVI. (*a*)), since 1884 at Bygdö, near Oslo, suggests more a ship with masts and tackle, and draws the eye to the central portion.

To the artistic value of height in the Norwegian churches is added the impression of lightness in contrast to the massive appearance of the block churches.   Of the latter, however, those with pyramidal roofs also draw attention to their height. In the mast-churches it is curious to note that the horizontal impression of the roofs arranged in steps has the same Chinese appearance as the eastern block churches.

A marked contrast between these two types of wood churches is shown in their interior form.   The principal types of block church are built up of an agglomeration of squares with a cupola.   In Norway the interior is an organic whole.

---

[1] Cf. also my book, *Der Norden in der bildenden Kunst Westeuropas*, pp. 37 *sq*.

PLATE XLIII

(b) Torpe Church: Detail of Roof

(a) Torpe Church, Hallingdal, Norway: Exterior View

PLATE XLIV

(a) Carved Panels at Urnes Church

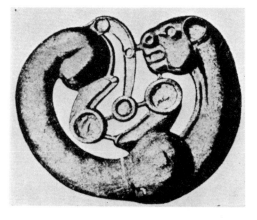

(b) Norwegian " Animal "
Ornament

(c) Siberian " Animal " Ornament
in Gold

A ship is not enlarged by the addition of another ship : so, too, a mast-church cannot be increased in size in the manner of a block church, by the addition of a further square with four masts.   It will be instructive to contrast with these types the third, having the essential features of the West European framework :   here, as in the southern basilica, the height is of no account.

The light in the interior is very similar in block churches and mast-churches.   The windows are very small, and the inside of the church is half in shadow.   It is interesting to recall that the early Christian Church favoured large windows and light.   May it not be that the changed taste was due to the northern wooden churches ?

From literary sources we hear of a gold roof or ceiling to the pagan hall or temple and coloured ornaments.   We found that the Croatian stone decoration showed colour, and it can be proved that colour was a feature of the block church also.

Ornament.—The ornament which we have seen on the doors of mast-churches at Borgund and other places appears to consist entirely of a mixture of the early North European band ornament with animal ornament, and the characteristic motives of the oriental art-stream which brought to Norway lions, dragons, and other animals.   These monuments are of a date later than 1200.   The only earlier building whose ornament we have studied is the church of Urnes, dating from about 1100, which seems to belong to a different era (Fig. 57).   It must be remembered that art is at its highest level in the North at the period which we have called in these chapters pre-Romanesque or North European.   The ornament at Urnes (Plate XLIV. (*a*)) consists of a remarkable scheme of lines derived from the movement of the animal's bodies, which are bordered by contour lines, the variation in the distance of which from the bodies corresponds to the thickness of the animal's limbs.   Thus the impression is conveyed that the body of the animal is present, but it cannot be defined except by Salin's method : there is one body clearly seen at Urnes on the left side of the door and the centre of the gable.

The architectural ornament in this early mast-church at Urnes is the finest example of mediæval art in Norway, and can only be explained as a development of an earlier pre-Christian art.   With this we shall deal in the last chapter.

In this place we are looking for artistic forms which bear the stamp of the northern spirit and not of imported motives, and it seems to me that this condition is fulfilled by the Urnes ornament.

5. *Content.*—The mast-churches can only be derived from certain personal qualities of the North Sea peoples. They are not a copy of church-types of other countries, but had their beginnings either, as I think, actually on the Scandinavian or, as Dietrichson suggests, elsewhere on the North Sea coast. They are an expression of the personality of the North Sea peoples at the times of the migrations of the Vikings. Personality did not enter into the discussions when we dealt with the churches of the countries where blockwork is found; but the mast-church has an individuality of its own. It may not be the individuality of a single person or a people, but it is at least that of the Teutonic area whose shipping is centred in the North Sea.

It would not greatly affect the study of the evolutionary development, if those scholars proved to be correct who consider that the " stave-church " type came with Christianity from the British Isles. This is not my own opinion, but British scholars will presumably deal with the subject more broadly than I can do. Whichever view be the right one, it is certain that the personality of which we spoke is that of the North Sea peoples : we shall revert to this point in the last chapter.

At present we are concerned only with the content of this church architecture and ornament. Is it the spirit of the Roman Church or that of a civilization unknown to those who trace everything to the South ? Certain scholars born in the North have tried to reconcile this art with the Roman or Romanesque forms. But the feeling is at once seen to be different, and it is without astonishment that we read in mast-churches inscriptions about 1200 Norwegian names, with legends such as " Thorolf made this church," or mere names written in runes—for example, Asgrim, Sigurd, Bärthor.

The quality of the ornament at Urnes was that of charm and liveliness, to such an extent that I cannot believe the artist to have been an imitator of foreign motives. What he has produced is his own northern art, of which he is a creator, in a tradition which he has inherited. It would not be surprising, therefore, to find in the decoration of the walls, door, or gable at Urnes one of the old Norwegian names written in runes.

III. Evolution.—It is clear that the type of the mediæval Norwegian church has no connection with the eastern blockwork, nor is it related to the western framework. These are both the outcome of a broad stream of art, the evolution of which covers hundreds or thousands of years. The church built with masts on sleepers enclosed by stave-screens and having a ship-like roof is apparently unique. Surely Diet-richson is in error when he suggests in his standard work, in which he is followed by the other orthodox art-historians, that this is simply a translation into wood of the Romanesque stone basilica, first (as at Urnes) with the characteristic details, especially the cube-capitals, but later becoming adapted gradually to the medium of wood. It is to be hoped that the discussion of the artistic values of this unique type has demonstrated the error of the humanistic theory, which later on, when the theories of the various investigators have been set forth, will reveal an extraordinary blindness on their part.

Attention must be drawn to a fact which we have hitherto not considered, namely, that the sleeper-and-mast churches, formerly known as " stave-churches," did not continue after the Reformation. Since that time all wooden churches have been built in blockwork, and the earlier mast-churches have been enlarged or restored by means of blockwork ; thus the block type which we studied in the second chapter was intro-duced into Norway.

This is a fact which cannot be explained, if we accept the theory that the mast-church is a translation into wood, with wooden columns, of the stone church ; stone churches and wooden churches continue to be built. If that theory were true, might it not mean that Norway dispensed with an art which was the source and origin of the artistic values found in the mast-church, namely, shipbuilding ? Let us consider this more particularly. Christianity came to Scandinavia in Viking times, when ships and shipbuilding were the channel into which flowed the ideas of the dwellers in the north-western corner of Europe, and the art of the North Sea peoples was focussed more upon the traffic from its shores than upon the interior of the countries forming this cultured area.

1. *Constant Elements in Mast-church Art.*—Was the mediæval church type in Norway in fact Norwegian ? In view of the fact that it was superseded, one might be tempted to think that it was not. Its discontinuance at the time of the Reforma-tion is not, I think, conclusive argument against a Norwegian origin, since the new orientation may have come from Finland,

Sweden, or Germany, countries employing the blockwork or framework technique.

I have already mentioned technical details which show affinity with shipbuilding. At this point a broader view may be taken of the problem, and we may inquire whether the art of shipbuilding did not exercise an influence from the beginning not only on the technique, but in general on architecture, first on pagan " halls " and later on Christian churches.

We know that one type of the pagan hall had a central mast. There are several allusions to this " firstsul." We are told that this type was suggested by such a building as the tenth century Visigothic church of San Baudel de Berlonga in Spain, a square of 8·5 × 9·5 m. with a single central column supporting an eight-ribbed roof of the early North European field and quarry stone (Plate XLVI. (b), (c)). Surely, however, the more natural prototype was a ship with its mast. Dietrich-son argues that the carpenter was initiated by the stone-mason into the work of church building, learning only by degrees the special qualities of the more elastic wood. This is the typical humanist view : the awkward and uncouth northerner ignorant of the properties of wood, and dependent on the superior wisdom of the South. And the belief is almost universal : the whole world, especially the barbarian North, learns from Greece and Rome ; knowledge resides solely in the Mediterranean cultural area. My experience, however, in the Asiatic east directly contradicts this view. The greatest art that we know in those regions reached its highest development before coming in any way into contact with what is known as classical art. Indeed, the countries on the northern frontier, such as Iran, lost their highly individual quality after the time of Alexander the Great. The same thing can be seen in the North of Europe, when the influence of Rome and the Roman Church begins to be felt. But I can offer these suggestions only as my own views, arrived at after many years of study and investigation ; and, as things are, I can hardly hope to secure much attention for the new orientation which I propose for scientific research. Evidence which is not Latin or Greek is suspect : it is merely the obsession of a confirmed Teutonist or anti-humanist, and cannot seriously be considered as interpreting or throwing light on monuments of the higher artistic value. A carpenter cannot be measured by the same standards as the builder in stone. I am filled

PLATE XLV

(a) Masted Church at Lomen, Norway

(b) Section of the Masted Church at Gol (cf. Fig. 65)

(c) Spalato Cathedral : The South Doorway

PLATE XLVI

(*a*) Church at Gol, Norway

(*b* and *c*) Details of Roof, Church of San Baudel de Berlanga, Spain

with a distrust of this doctrine established by education and a continuous tradition.

Hitherto we have shown small interest in shipbuilding. The art-histories have neglected it. To-day, as we contemplate the luxurious appointments of our transatlantic liners, we may give a thought to the art which contributed to our comfort on the voyage, but how many are aware that the building of ships helped to determine the development of architecture, and especially of church architecture?

Where could such an influence be found? Surely on the coast of the North Sea. In the old Hibernian and Icelandic sagas the scene is laid in places in which human activities centre round ships and shipping. What could be more natural, then, than that Christianity, coming to Norway in the Viking period, should itself turn to shipbuilding as a model for church architecture?

FIG. 61.—PLAN OF THE CHURCH AT NES (NORWAY).

Fig. 61 shows a church (Nes) which seems at least to suggest the work of the shipbuilder. There is a central mast

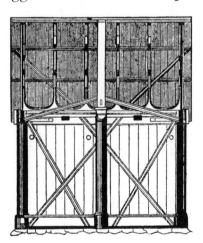 

FIG. 62.—DETAILS OF CONSTRUCTION IN THE CHURCH AT FLAA (NORWAY).

fixed as follows: The point at which two sleepers cross gives a solid foundation for the mast. On the four ends of the sleepers thin screens are erected to enclose the interior area; these screens cannot be heavy as they are to be supported by the sleepers. Thus we have a technique like that of the shipbuilder: screens of upright boards between two sleepers, of which one is lower than the other, but fixed by four pillars in the corners. The screens of such a church cannot bear the whole weight of the roof, which muſt be taken in part by the walls. The church of Nes illuſtrates this. The walls are connected with the central maſt by four beams from the middle of the upper edge of the walls.

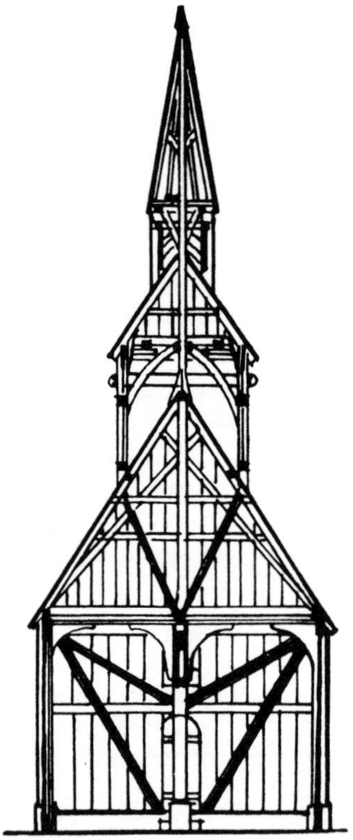

By means of them the maſt is enabled to support a ſtrong beam, as shown in the church at Flaa (Fig. 62). The roof is not a pyramid over a square, but gabled with sloping roofs; the maſt may exceed the roof in height, and at Nes (Fig. 63) it supports a small belfry.

It is evident that such a technique is impossible in blockwork or in weſtern framework. The "firſtsul" mentioned in legal and other documents may perhaps be connected in some way with the single-maſt technique in some Norwegian churches. But, generally speaking, it is contrary to the essential principle of framework to concentrate a building round one pillar. What of Norway itself? Dietrichson calls this type of church the "Numedal" type, and considers that it belongs to the end of the period, as it is often found along with the pointed arch of the second half of the thirteenth century. It has been mentioned that he considers the maſt-church a simplified adaptation to wood architecture of the Roman ſtone basilica, beginning with numerous maſts, and reduced as the carpenter becomes familiar with the properties of his medium to four. How is the reduction to one maſt to be explained? Dietrichson's opinion is that the reason for this curious feature is the desire to preserve the small belfry in the roof, which, with its swinging bell, is to be supported by the centre maſt.

FIG. 63.—SECTION OF THE CHURCH AT NES.

In the illustration of the church of Borgund, and on the other churches, you find the small belfry. The steeple marking the apex of the perpendicular axis appears to be a relic of the time when the only type was the one-mast church. That is my explanation, the height and the perpendicular axis being the predominating architectural value, with a secondary axis like that of the second sleeper crossing the one for the fixing of the mast.

The earliest monument of this type is Flaa in Hallingdal, in the diocese of Oslo, dating from about 1200, the first mention of it being in 1327; it was destroyed in 1854. It measured 25 × 17 feet, the height of the screen being 15 feet, and of the roof 27 feet. As in the oldest extant church (from 1100), the single mast had a cube-capital : there was no belfry. The details all show the shipbuilding technique, especially in the inverted arches separating the rafters on the roof.

2. *Political and National Influences.*—Dietrichson is convinced that the " stave-church " was introduced into Norway along with Christianity, both coming from the British Isles. He has no doubt that both emanated from the same country, and he has to determine upon a country in order to distinguish the Norwegian features in the building and ornament. He forgets, however, that shortly before the eleventh century wood building was practised in all the northern countries, and it is not surprising to read of the church of S. Kentigern, in Wales, in the sixth century, that it was built *more Britonum, quum de lapide nondum construere poterant, nec usum habuerant.*

One kind of wood building was called *opus Scoticum* or *mos Scoticarum gentium.* According to Dietrichson, this type is the " stave " building seen at Greenstead. I cannot pronounce upon this, but, as I have shown, the essential features of Norwegian wood architecture are not staves, but sleepers and masts. There is no part of the world where this technique can be found but Norway; it is not due to the dictates of missionaries, but is a constant element.

Until we have studied the existing material for the western framework type of wooden church we cannot come to a definite conclusion about it.

It is a remarkable fact that neither Romanesque nor Gothic art, introducing the influence of the international church, could drive out the enduring tradition of the mast-church. It persisted in Norway at a time of great and monumental stone churches, and only ceased in the sixteenth century from some cause not yet explained.

3. *Development from Earlier Forms.*—It is surely possible that this unique mast-church is indigenous, but derived from other structures, to which the technique of sleepers and masts, screens to enclose the area, and sloping roofs on the model of a ship, was appropriate. I suggested the possibility that the hall, especially the royal hall, and the temple, might become the assembly hall of believers and the Christian House of God. There would thus be a simple transition similar to the transformation of the ancient Greek dwelling-house and the palace (μέγαρον) to the house of God, first in wood then in stone, the sole difference being that the wooden church was the last stage in Norway itself, no translation into stone, in my opinion, having ever taken place.

At this point I am tempted to make a slight digression. If the origin of the Greek temple was a building similar to the mast-church, the idea is suggested of a building with the pairs of sleepers crossing but with the masts fixed, not at the points of crossing between which the four walls would stand, but on the end of the sleepers. The idea is doubtless an extravagant one, but some treatment of the origin of the Greek temples seems to be called for. What type of wood building is at the beginning of this movement? Is it the northern peasant's dwelling which we consider to be the prototype?

It seems to me to be more than a mere chance that we can locate the centre of mast-church building in that part of the European North which has the largest extent of sea coast in the western cultural area of the North Sea region. Further, the Numedal valley, the home of the single-masted church, is situated in the immediate neighbourhood of the old diocese of Oslo: again, it is hardly an accident that to this place we can attribute the church type that has the closest affinity with shipbuilding. And it seems to have been precisely in Oslo that shipbuilding was most highly developed, a fact which appears from several excavations of pre-Christian ship-graves on both sides of the Oslo Fjord. With these we shall be concerned in the last chapter.

CHAPTER V.

ROYAL TOMBS IN SCANDINAVIA.

It is a remarkable fact that while attention is concentrated on discoveries in the South—the tomb of Tut-ankh-amen is the latest obsession—there is no mention of a monument in the North which has been known since 1904 and is of equal importance and artistic value : it is a royal tomb found in a tumulus and, like that of Tut-ankh-amen, showing the deceased persons surrounded by the furniture used by them in everyday life. The objects found in this northern hill are to-day treasured proudly by the Norwegian people, and occupy a number of rooms in the University Museum at Oslo. These are not the relics of a people and civilization several thousands of years old and unrelated to ourselves : this royal tomb of the North, by reason of the geographical situation and its influence on the race that built the tomb, is a product of our own ancient northern civilization, and is little more than one thousand years old. Few are aware of this ; but it is surely the duty of northern peoples to give some thought to the treasures of the North.

The reason for our neglecting our own northern monuments, regardless of their artistic worth, is, as we have seen before, the humanistic prepossession : the northern peoples are barbarians, and derive architecture and the graphic arts from the South, the fount of culture. This was accepted as an article of faith centuries ago, and has blinded us to the creative artistry of the North in early times.

In my studies on the origin of Christian art, it was in Asia, in the art of Iran, that I first discovered a powerful rival to the culture of Greece and Rome, and it is from that country, situated on the southern part of Northern Asia, that the art known to us as mediæval, was derived. Later, however, I saw that this Iranian world was closely related to the North of Europe, and that to understand the one it was necessary to be acquainted with the other. Thus I was obliged to return

by a new way of my own from my studies in Inner Asia to
Europe. I found myself not at Rome or Byzantium, from
which I had started, but on the coasts of the North and Baltic
Seas.

As an historian of Christian art, I go back not to pre-
historic times, but to the centuries shortly before and after the
year 1000, to the beginnings of Christianity on the Continent
and in Scandinavia, a region of the North Sea which might
be called the centre of the Teutonic peoples. There foreign
influences could not in a moment destroy or even seriously
disturb the culture of the northern race that settled in the
north-western corner of Europe, between the Celts and the
Slavs. From this centre the Teutonic peoples again moved
towards the West and the South, after the fall of the Roman
Empire. The Celts, who were already under the domination
of the Roman·emperors, formed a second line behind the
western Goths and the Franks, while Britain had fallen into
the hands of the Anglo-Saxons. This was prior to the immigration of the Lombards into Italy ; but the historian must
bear in mind that the Lombards not only came to Italy later,
but left their northern settlements earlier than the Anglo-
Saxons and Franks, and lived for some time in the countries
of the Carpathians before moving towards Italy. This we
pointed out in dealing with Croatian art.

It is the second and later movement in the northern area
that will specially concern us in this chapter, a maritime
movement with the North Sea in particular as its centre. In
the Carolingian period the Vikings sailed in quest of treasure
on the west coast of Europe, and the Normans were capturing
territory in France and England, finally becoming Kings of
Sicily. The tomb which we are about to consider is no
ordinary unadorned grave, but that of a Viking princess or
queen.

Before proceeding to the study of this monument, we
should bear in mind the high standard of Anglo-Saxon and
Hibernian art. It is a strange fact, and one which seems at
first hardly credible, that, having observed the flourishing
Christian art of the British Isles, when we come to Scandinavia,
we must return to paganism, and that while Great Britain was
becoming more and more absorbed by Roman Church art,
and the old Irish and Anglo-Saxon art was disappearing, there
was still to be found in the far North a centre of Teutonic art
untouched by outside influences. To-day it is represented

only by the monumental tombs of the Viking period, though once, no doubt, the wooden temples and royal halls stood there, of which the Song of Beowulf, the two Eddas, and the Icelandic sagas gave an impressive account but an imperfect idea.[1]

I. Study of the Monuments.—At this point attention must be drawn to one of the most important pagan centres of the early Teutonic world, Gamla Upsala in Sweden, in which are three hills, 60 metres in diameter and 18 metres high, called the Hills of the Kings, or, in the popular nomenclature, known as the Hills of Odin, Thor, and Freyr.   In the neighbourhood of Upsala will be found also the cemetery of Vendel, with its boat-graves, which leads us to a type of monument which we shall have to discuss in this chapter—the great ship-graves. They are preserved not in Sweden but in Norway, although the Kings of the Vikings probably took the model from the Svea-Kings.   In the Odins-hög, near Upsala, the grave of King Aun the Old, about 500 B.C., were excavated traces of a burnt ship, similar finds being recorded in other countries, including the British Isles, to which Scandinavian sailors penetrated.   The belief that after death men sailed to the islands of the blest led to the burial of the body in the boat, along with such provisions for the voyage as might be required after death, a similar custom to that observed in Egypt.

The first discoveries were made on the east side of the Oslo Fiord in 1751, the first great ship was found in a hill in Rolfs-Öy, and in 1867 the June-ship was discovered in Haugen.   Both were royal tombs of the Vestfold family, monuments built, as experts have proved, on the regular traditional lines of Norse paganism.   Later, on the west side of the same fiord, were found other graves of greater interest for us.   In 1852 excavations on a hill in Borre disclosed a

[1] There is a strong case for the early institution of a Teutonic museum in England.   In America Harvard University possesses a museum which goes by the name of the Germanic Museum, but the visitor will find that it consists merely of gesso casts of all the mediæval statues and reliefs in Germany.   If it is urged that the time is not ripe for a Teutonic museum in England, the answer is that at a time when Spengler and others are writing books showing that the ultimate fall of Europe is inevitable, we should inquire into the artistic state of Europe before the Roman and Byzantine churches established the styles which we call Byzantine, Romanesque, Gothic, Renaissance, and so forth.   This would give us a fresh point of view and would be the best way of clearing our minds of the obsession which has taken so firm a hold of European thought.

ship 17 metres long, made for a wealthy chief, and containing three horses. In 1880 the Gokstad ship was brought to light, 22·80 metres in length ; it was also built for a chief, and contained sixteen horses, sixteen dogs, and a peacock. These discoveries, however, were far surpassed in interest by Gustafson's discovery in 1904 at a place called Oseberg, and it is the main object of the present chapter to show the importance of the art of this Oseberg ship. Plate LII. (*b*) shows part of the ornament on the roof of the small burial chamber found in the Gokstad ship, an animal's head in a solid style with fine band ornament.

We may now proceed to the description of the Oseberg ship. It is built of oak, and was apparently intended for use. It is 21·44 metres in length, and 5·10 metres in breadth, with seventeen ribs, displacing about 11,000 kilogrammes of water. To the rear of the pinewood mast, now 5·70 metres high, was found a small burial chamber, as on the other ships. The chamber differs from those found on the other ships in containing two female skeletons. The entire deck was filled with household furniture [1] of the most sumptuous character.

Fig. 64 (*a*) is taken from the standard work, *Osebergfundet utgit av den norske stat*, by Drs. Brögger, Falk, and Shetelig, in five volumes, of which three have now appeared, which the Norwegian Government began to publish in 1917. It shows the longitudinal section. The ship is seen embedded in the hill. When the ship had been covered with field-stones, the mound was erected over it. The bottom of the ship is almost entirely destroyed, especially in the middle, so that the burial chamber behind the mast is unduly sunk and quite out of shape : the beam connecting the top of the lateral posts is broken. It was found by Gustafson that the tomb, like that of Tut-ankh-amen, had been visited at an earlier period by thieves, who had destroyed the wall of the chamber and cut off both of the queen's hands to secure the jewels.

In Fig. 64 (*b*) is shown the ground plan of the ship and the

---

[1] Now occupying an entire floor of the University Museum at Oslo. Norwegian scholars have spared no pains to restore the damaged and half-decayed treasures, and have taken endless trouble and shown untiring patience in preserving and exhibiting the objects to the best advantage. The finest specimens are preserved in running water. In 1916 the Storthing resolved to erect a great hall to accommodate all Viking ships, which had hitherto been preserved in the open-air museum of Bygdö, near Oslo.

hill, which illustrates the proportions and position of the ship. In the stern is the helm, and at the other end the anchor, the small burial chamber and the mast being amidships.

Plate XLVII. illustrates the ship after it had been cleared of earth and stones, and before the separation of the various

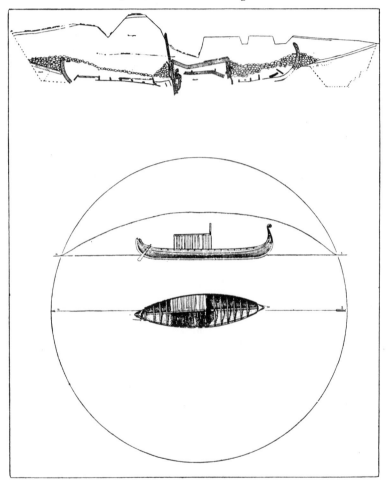

FIG. 64 (*a*).—OSEBERG SHIP : LONGITUDINAL SECTION.
(*b*).—OSEBERG SHIP : POSITION OF THE SHIP IN THE HILL.

articles of household furniture. Single objects cannot be distinguished here, and the laborious nature of the task may be imagined. First of all drawings were made of the objects of natural size, after which facsimiles were carved by an artist named Ericson : the single pieces were kept, and it was only then that the experts could attempt to piece the fragments together. The northern climate is less favourable to the preservation of wooden objects than the dry sand of Egypt; if all the decorative wooden sculpture could have been preserved in the North as it has been in the deserts of Egypt and Central Asia, there would be less cause for wonder in the widespread craftsmanship of which some idea is given by the Oseberg ship and the stave-churches.

The burial chamber of the Oseberg ship disclosed two female skeletons, one of a queen or princess of forty or fifty years of age, lying on the coverings of a bed; the other probably a servant of perhaps thirty years old. The room was furnished with rich textiles.

The appearance of these skeletons may be imagined to some extent if we call to mind the well-known Hegesos relief, one of the finest specimens of Hellenic art, of about 390 B.C. Here in the work of a northern sculptor in southern marble, more than a thousand years before that which we are studying, we can form some idea of the bodies of the Norwegian queen and her servant.

On the deck of the ship in front and in rear of the mast and the burial chamber was found the store of fine household furniture, which constitutes the greatest treasure of purely northern art which we possess. I propose first to give comprehensive descriptions of various objects, and later to describe the ornament. On the after-deck was a kitchen: a kettle with the accompanying paraphernalia was outside the burial chamber, as were also a mill and a hatchet, and on the steersman's seat the remains of an ox. The decorated objects were found in front of the mast: first, a carriage, four sledges, then three beds, one chair, three tents, parts of walls with shelves, a wooden bucket, a stick with a runner, shoes, a spade, a barrel, the skeletons of fifteen horses and four dogs, and other objects. I shall deal only with the carriage and the sledges, photographs of which are reproduced by the kind permission of the keeper of the University Oldsagsamling. They are not all built in the same way: we may note, for example, the clumsy locks of the carriage (Plate XLVIII. (a)), the heavy wheels with their thick hubs, the rounded spokes and broad felloes in six or seven sections. On the axles are seen two long beams over which are two supports sustaining a kind of trough. The carriage is so crude and heavily-built that we may suppose that it was only designed to be drawn by cattle over bad roads, a true carriage of Nerthus.

PLATE XLVII

Oslo: The Oseberg Ship, in its excavated bed

PLATE XLVIII

(a) Carriage from the Oseberg Ship

(b) Oseberg Ship : The Second Sledge

(c) Oseberg Ship : The Fourth Sledge

A wholly different impression is given by the three sledges. In contrast to the carriage they are very lightly built in the lower part, and each with its own special design. The second sledge (Plate XLVIII. (*b*)), to use present-day terminology, has runners curved on one side only. In the sledge itself are to be seen three pairs of supports connected by two beams carrying a rectangular box consisting of four boards fixed in corner-posts. The third sledge (Plate XLIX. (*a*)) has a similar box but is heavier still in contrast to the sledge itself, which is slender, and more quadrangular in shape, with slanting sides resting on the rear portion. The fourth sledge (Plate XLVIII. (*c*)) shows the same finished workmanship; the box is lower and placed just over the centre of the sledge.

At the outset it may have seemed that the point of interest for us was not the construction of the ship, carriage, and sledges, but the ornament, seeing that the humanistic tyranny which refuses to recognize antique art not based on classical models [1] has withheld recognition from the so-called " primitive " Teutonic art, in which the human figure is not represented.

For many years now we have recognized two kinds of pictorial art—the Southern, in which the human figure appears ; and the Northern, in which it is not shown. The North, as long as it was true to its essential character, renounced the human figure in art : it delighted above all in conventional ornament, and this feeling for ornament was combined with the employment of certain symbols which were of frequent occurrence in the Christian art of the North, just as they are to-day throughout the religious art of Islam. The South before the Greek migrations had none of this love of artistic expression for its own sake ; they drew art into the service of the court, and the church, or used it for some doctrinal purpose. Later on this type frequently imposed its will upon the North. The iconoclastic movements implied a reaction of the northern blood, and the non-representational character of Mohammedan religious art has its origin on the frontier of the Asiatic north in Iran.

The ornament on our early Norwegian carriage and on the sledges well exemplifies northern art. Many who do not

[1] I am reminded that when asked in Washington about my impressions of America, I replied quite seriously that I was surprised to see in the American Art Museum no specimens of ancient American art. The observation excited no interest.

realize the interconnection of the various countries and artistic
tendencies in the history of art may say that this ornament has
an Islamic appearance.   This is certainly so, as I have already
shown in my *Altai-Iran and the Migrations*, 1917, and the art-
treasures of the Oseberg ship have striking affinities with the
wood and stucco works from the east of the Mohammedan
world.   The direct connection is possible, and is proved by
the great numbers of silver coins of East Iranian dynasties
of the tenth century, found in the European North.   Non-
representational art must have been from the beginning
indigenous to the North of Europe and Asia.   It is also to be
remembered that northern peoples like the Greeks or Indians
had already brought to the representational art of the South
the new formal values of the running scroll.

Turning now to the ornament on the Oseberg ship and
on the carriages and sledges found in it, we realize that they
are carved in a material in which ordinarily we take no
pleasure—that is to say, not in marble, alabaster, or any other
such medium, but in wood.   Why should we show a preference for the South, Egypt, or Crete ? We are surely not mere
lovers of precious metals or the like, who estimate the worth
of an object by the intrinsic value of its material : we are lovers
of art who see beauty in any fine work, whatever the medium.
If the state of civilization is a simple one, we are interested in
the spiritual values, the culture.   Where has a higher culture
been found than in ancient Egypt, thousands of years before
Christ ; or in the second half of the first millennium of our era,
in the artistic area of the North Sea countries ?

The ship is decorated on the stern and on the keel.   Plate
XLIX. (*b*) shows the ornament on the bow, and attention
may be drawn to the way in which it is placed in its setting.
On the left side there is a smooth surface with a narrow
border of lines followed by the actual ornament carved
separately, the surface being afterwards roughened.   The
ornament consists of interlaced animals, the head of one
appearing in the body of the adjoining animal, in which two
perforations are always found.   This is a fundamental point
in the entire scheme of decoration on the ship.   A second
point is that the surface of the animal's body shows various
patterns ; and, thirdly, the feet, tail, and ears become thin
lines, following the lines of the animal's body in a scheme of
great variety and delicacy.

In Plate XLIX. (*c*) may be seen a second example of the

PLATE XLIX

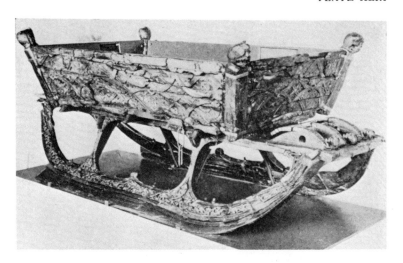

(*a*) Oseberg Ship   The Third Sledge

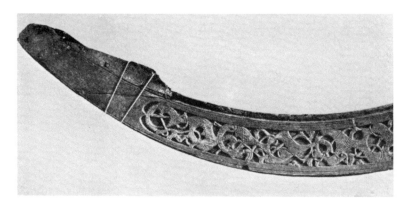

(*b*) Oseberg Ship : Detail of Carved Ornament from the Ship itself

(*c*) Oseberg Ship   Detail of Carved Ornament

PLATE L

(*a*) Oseberg Ship : Ornament on the Carriage

(*b*) Oseberg Ship : Ornament on the Third Sledge

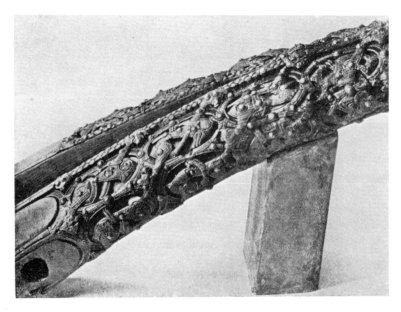

(*c*) Oseberg Ship : Carved Ornament on a pole

ornament on the ship, one of the ribs securing the sides of the ship. Two figures with human heads and animal bodies are shown symmetrically placed: the hair (ears ?) extends in the form of lines along the body, intersecting the animal motive.

Coming to the ornament on the carriage (Plate XLVIII. (a)) we see that the two bifurcating pieces supporting the trough terminate in fantastic animal or human heads. The ornament on the trough is a good example of *horror vacui*. One end of the trough is illustrated (Plate L. (a)); the angles at the base are rounded; on the top is a cable border; in the field are numerous figures of animals regularly disposed so as to fill the space in the manner of flat ornament. Here the animals are otherwise represented than on the ship. They do not lie in an interlaced pattern on the ground: each animal is separated from the other, although they are shown in combat. Unfortunately the boards are split and many parts of the ornament are destroyed. On the left a man is struggling with serpents which completely surround him: he grasps them with both hands, at the same time repelling them with his feet; one is seen on his body, and another is biting him. On the left is a creature resembling a lizard. The head of the man should be observed with the large cavity in the place of the ear, the beard, and the wig-like hair.

Round this Norse Laocoon, who may perhaps be identified by Teutonic scholars, may be seen animals of various sorts disposed in horizontal lines. To the right of the first man a second holds the legs of an animal above his head. At his right hand is a group consisting of birds, animals, and serpents; and underneath, an oblique pattern of animals in groups; in the right-hand corner is a group of animals in motion. The designs on the bodies are not so rough, and the patterns formed by contour lines to the legs are characteristic. These patterns are roughly executed and arbitrarily planned, and seem to be the work of a carver whose only aim is to occupy the field with a regular design. It will be seen that the opposite end of the carriage (Plate L. (a)) is the counterpart of that which we have described, and shows animals in combat; these, however, have female heads with pointed ears. On the sides of the trough may be seen animals fighting, with bodies sometimes ornamented with interlaced bands of two striations; here, too, an exception is to be noted—two human figures (one like the man with the serpent) and a man on horseback. It is, perhaps, conceivable that both scenes, and the animals in combat, may have some reference to the destination of the carriage.

The decoration of the sledges may now be considered. It is more rigidly conventional, and figure-subjects are absent on the sides of the boxes. The pure geometrical ornament predominates to such an extent that it is actually more noticeable than the animal motives seen on the corner-posts of the bodies, on the runners, and on the poles. The second sledge (Plate XLVIII. (b)) is ornamented with different varieties of lozenge patterns on the sides of the body. Metal studs are seen at the points of intersection of the lozenges. On each corner-post is an animal head bell-shaped, and the posts are decorated throughout with interlaced and pierced animal ornament, giving a fantastic appearance to the whole.

The third sledge (Plate XLIX. (a)) is the most interesting for art-history. The framework of the lower part is suggestive from the technical point of view : it has animal ornament, and trefoil motives are seen on the triangular terminals to the supports. These were discussed in my book on Croatia, pp. 166-7. In contrast to the light framework of the lower part is the very heavy box-shaped body, which attracts the eye only by reason of its decoration. The heads on the corners, suggesting those of bull-dogs, have a truculent appearance. The ornaments on the sides illustrate a fundamental value of Norse art. Below the higher plane with geometrical rectilinear designs there appear on a lower plane carved lines in a kind of scroll pattern. In the detail of the shorter sides of the body, illustrated in Plate L. (b), three planes may be clearly distinguished. The first plane alternately framed by a border of projecting studs, circular and rhomboid, shows a continuous pattern of contiguous semi-circles with small circles or rhombs at the points of contact ; the second plane a cross with rectangular arms ; while the third, on the ground, is made up of interlaced bands smooth on the surface and of varying thickness.

The fourth sledge (Plate XLVIII. (c)) has the richest ornament. Some details are shown, but, unfortunately, not from the corner-posts with the heads and roughly studded surface border with interlaced scrolls. Plate LI. (b) shows one of the shorter ends of the box, the upper part of which is ornamented with beading and scroll-work like that of the corner-posts. The field shows, in the first plane, a lozenge pattern with the sides of the rhombs hatched, and with metal studs at the points

of intersection.   In the second plane another network consisting of the most characteristic of the animal motives.   This
box is particularly striking by reason of the contrast of rough
with smooth polished bands once enhanced with colours.
The ornament on the lower part of the sledge (Plate LI. (*a*))
has more the appearance of being on a single plane.   Plate
XLVIII. (*c*) shows the structural excellence of the supports,
and it will be noticed that the sledge increases in breadth in
the lower part.   The junction of the edge of the runner to the
upper part of the support is buttressed, so to speak, by
triangular pieces carved with animal ornament (cf. Plate LI. (*a*)).
Notice the fine curve of the lower part in the direction of the
upper board.   Between both is a spherical piece carved as a
human mask.   The ornament of the lower part consists of
circles of various sizes, with two striations, interlaced with
very curious animal motives.   In the middle is seen a figure
resembling a rampant heraldic animal to left.   On the upper
border of three stripes, on the right, is what appears to be
a grinning human mask.   The whole design is enriched by
metal studs.

    In Plate LI. (*a*) a difference of treatment may be observed
between the upper and lower parts.   On the lower part the
ornament stands on a background only visible in small
patches ; on the upper part the surface of the wood is smooth
and without ornament on the sides.   This formal value was
first introduced by the Greeks to the South, and it is strikingly
employed in the carriages and sledges which we are considering, and especially in the decoration of the poles at their
extremities.

    A pole of this kind is illustrated in Plate L. (*c*).   On the
left may be seen two pieces of triangular section meeting on
the right in the shaft.   The former end in two arches separating the smooth surface from the richly ornamented portion.
The ornament consists of large ovals with hatched borders
and metal studs.   The border above is pearled, and ornamented
with studs ; at intervals along this border appear animal heads
as terminals to bodies within the ovals, and continuing trans-
versely over them.   There is a still richer example, with interlaced animal ornament in four planes, published in my
Altai-Iran (p. 209).

    We have not so far considered in detail the animal heads
on the corners of the sledge-boxes.   I have reserved this for
the end of my description of the Oseberg ship, in view of the

unsurpassed richness and liveliness of the ornament.   The two last examples (Plate LII. (*a*), (*c*)) give an admirable illustration of the contrast between the smooth and the decorated surfaces.   The distribution is different on the two " dragonsticks."   In the one (Plate LII. (*a*)) the lower end is smooth while the entire upper part is richly ornamented.   The neck and the head have interlaced animal designs, the head showing the fondness for the strap-work motive, which is seen in the ear.   The eyes and nose project in the form of bosses, and the face has a chessboard pattern.   The open mouth with the teeth is apparently indicated by a perforation.   The second stick (Plate LII. (*c*)) seems to me to be one of the most noble creations among all the woodwork of the Oseberg ship.   The neck is left smooth for the most part, but at the base is a broad band with a pattern of smooth bosses enclosed in squares with sides of three striations.   As in the other examples, the expression of the animal is menacing, in spite of the fact that the ears and teeth are broken off.   As a work of art it is full of character, and a fine effect is given by the contrast of the smooth surfaces of the eyes, nose, and lips, with the carving on the rest of the head.   Is this typical of a primitive or barbaric art?

II. The Essential Character of Shipbuilding, and Ornament in the Viking Period.—The monuments which we have been studying are unique in the history of art, and it may be that England is the country in which their merits will be first recognized and appreciated.   It must be evident that shipbuilding in the Viking period was possessed of an austerity which gave it a peculiar character all its own.   It is a grateful task not only to describe the monument as we see it, but to appreciate its art and technique and their seeming essential interdependence ;   which would be a step towards filling the most unfortunate blank in the history of early North European art, the wooden monuments which preceded Roman and Christian architecture and the historical period in the North.

Shipbuilding is the branch of wood-technique which demands the most careful and exact workmanship, as we have seen from comparison with the early churches of blockwork and framework, and the mast-churches, with sleepers and masts.   It is therefore hardly an accident that in the busiest centres of ship-designing and building, as, for example, on the Oslo Fiord and on the Scandinavian coasts generally, in the Finnish Oesterbotten, and on the Dalmatian coast, a conspicuous and relatively advanced art may be found.

PLATE LI

(a) Oseberg Ship: Ornament on the Fourth Sledge

(b Oseberg Ship   Ornament on the Fourth Sledge

PLATE LII

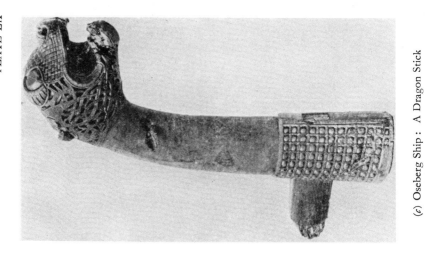

(c) Oseberg Ship : A Dragon Stick

(b) Oslo : Detail from the Gokstad Ship

(a) Oseberg Ship : A Dragon Stick

1. *Raw Materials and Technique.*—We have already dealt with the mast-churches, suggesting that the explanation of this singular North Sea type of church might be found in shipbuilding. We are now happily in a position to state the case from the other side. In the same country we have preserved a great collection of ships, some of the highest artistic merit, especially the Oseberg ship. Here we have at once an illustration of wood furniture with its characteristic ornament of interlaced bands. Before the discovery of the Oseberg ship our knowledge of northern art was confined to metal-work in various materials, gold, silver, and a large quantity of bronze. As I pointed out many years ago, these are not the principal materials for the art-historian. He cannot use the sub-divisions of pre-history, Stone Age, Bronze Age, and Iron Age. These raw materials are of secondary importance, and evolution in Northern Europe can only be traced in wood ; or in Asia in unburnt brick or the tent. Pre-historians, like historians, are concerned only with the extant monuments. The expert researcher in art-history is conscious of the unfilled blanks, and takes account of them.

The fallacy persists that building in wood indicates a primitive peasant art : this prejudice is probably responsible for its neglect by the historians of art, who consider the association of the words " wood " and " architecture " essentially absurd. We may in turn ask whether the shipbuilding of the Viking period is not wood-architecture ; indeed, by reason of its high art it is the one branch accepted by my colleagues in art-history. If this be allowed, are not the mast-churches and the half-timber and block-churches also architecture in the truest sense of the word ?

What, it may be asked, constitutes architecture ? It is perhaps inexpedient to defy the humanists to the extent of asserting that all " architecture " comes from the North, and was at one time wood architecture. But at least we may suggest that to regard stone and brick as the only true raw materials of architecture may be a short-sighted view. What proof is there that stone and brick were originally the principal raw materials ? It may perhaps be answered that the round building is certainly of stone origin, that it is the mark of Mediterranean art, with the Pantheon as its chief representative. But the Greek temple is built on the same plan as the northern house ; and have not the details of the Doric and Ionic styles, and the cupola on a square, wooden prototypes ?

We discussed this in the second chapter, where it was further shown that barrel vaults appeared not only on Mesopotamian brick buildings, but also, however strange it might seem, in wood architecture.

We may then compromise with the humanists by suggesting that art-history must face the possibility that in the North wood was the chief raw material for architecture and ornament. It is not unnatural that we can most easily prove the supreme importance of wood from the stone and brick monuments of the South, since, in the first place, the northern originals are lost on account of the perishable nature of the wood and the wet climate of the North, and, secondly, the northern peoples moving southward brought with them northern wood architecture which served as models for stone and brick buildings, of which evidence is derived from the Iranians, Indians, Greeks, Armenians, Croatians, and Western Goths.

We are now concerned with the technique of shipbuilding. Here we may perhaps expect to find motives which became important in the evolution of architecture. Mention may be made especially of parallel ribs, or spans, which in pointed or keel-shaped arches constituting roofs resemble an inverted ship (Fig. 65). Similar constructions are found in West European framework buildings, but it is the technique of shipbuilding that demands the accuracy and security in which the timber-yards foreshadow the later " Gothic " workshops of the stone-masons.

Coming to ornament, we may ask what is exactly meant by the term. Ornament is, it may also be said, found in Africa, the ancient centre of the southern movement. There, however, as in the neighbouring European and Asiatic peninsulas, representation of the human form is predominant. That is the native art there, just as to the North geometrical ornament without the human figure is indigenous. If, as it would seem, there is a certain appropriateness in the northern use of ornament to decorate a surface, is not wood of some importance in connection with its building utility? It is less heavy than stone, and its constructive technique may perhaps call for greater craftsmanship. Northern art arose mainly from craftsmanship, while the South favoured representational art. Therefore pure ornament founded on geometrical designs, such as we have seen on the early Croatian stone furniture and in the Oseberg ship, was originally the only art known to the European North.

2. *Significance.*—Ship architecture and ornament are not generally regarded as being in the same category as churches and palaces. In the latter case, utility is not considered, having, as the humanists assert, nothing to do with art. The problem is the same as that which arises from the consideration of raw material, especially in connection with wood. A ship is built primarily with a view to utility : the ships excavated from Viking graves are built for use like the Oseberg ship. Is it then a work of art ? Modern engineers and connoisseurs of art conversant with engineering problems will readily find

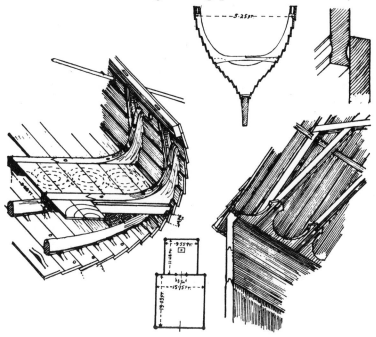

FIG. 65.—SHIPBUILDING MOTIVES ADAPTED TO TIMBER CONSTRUCTION IN CHURCH BUILDINGS (*cf.* Plate XLV.·(*b*)).

an answer. The questions underlying modern criticism were introduced by Semper into art-history. If we are to answer them is it not time for us to study them from the historical and geographical point of view, as they have been viewed already from the æsthetic side ? A strong incentive to such research is given by the new materials from the European North.

Up to the time of the migrations, ornament in the North of Europe was since its initial stage evolved from handicrafts, and was, as I showed, geometrical. Now shipbuilding and furniture at their most flourishing period show interlaced band and animal ornament. We have spoken of its origin in various parts of Northern Asia; but it may possibly have also expressed the taste of the sailor. We know that the ornament on the stem of the ship (Plate LII. (*b*)) also appeared in private houses, and that in this way the dragon may possibly have found its way as a favourite motive into the decoration of the hall, temple, and church.

3. *Shape.*—Shipbuilding has certainly its own shapes, which in general are not closely akin to those of the house or hall, or the temple or church building. But in the North-West European corner of the North Sea we know of a highly developed shipbuilding which seems to supply the model for what we call the mast-church, and perhaps was responsible for the ready acceptance of animal ornament. It seems possible, therefore, that certain shapes found in shipbuilding are of importance in the future development of wood architecture.

A. *Architecture.*—In Roman times there are found a single vault with long turned barrels or with barrels intersecting over a square, and with the cupola over the round plan or the octagon. Romanesque and, still more, Gothic art employed rows of parallel bays along the main axis separated at first by transverse arches, and later by crossing ribs. Now this architectural scheme has its origin in early North European wood architecture: the germ of it is found in western framework and northern shipbuilding with spans. This is a shape, as I have already pointed out in dealing with the technique, which is most apparently derived also from shipbuilding. It is not only the roof of the mast-church, but also the triforium and other details that are related to this art, so long neglected by historians of art. We must now pass to the subject of ornament, which is more important for the purposes of this chapter.

B. *Ornament.*—I pointed out that southern art was representational and portrayed the human figure; northern art is more formal, employing linear ornaments. Only once, by exception, have we met with the human figure in the decoration of the box of the carriage, and it will be agreed that in general it is unrepresented in early northern art. Art-historians claim that non-representational art is primitive art on the ground that the naturalistic portrayal of the human body at rest or in motion is unknown. It is certain, however, that the rich interlaced animal and band ornament on the ship and the sledges cannot be dismissed as primitive art.

The animal ornament on the ships is that which we have found also on the maſt-churches, but on the ship at an earlier and, what is all-important, a higher ſtage of artiſtic evolution. The firſt appearance of the animal in Northern European art was in the age called by the prehiſtorian the Bronze Age. We do not know the form it then took in wood. But all the forms which we have now found to be charaĉteriſtic of the migration and Viking periods, the interlaced ſtrap, the movements of the animals, etc., seem to be of Asiatic origin.

4. *Form.*—The ship-form is not a type which we commonly ſtudy, like a façade or an interior. The ship was in Viking times the open-air habitation of a body of men, to be set in motion by human power. I lay ſtress on the words, " set in motion." With the church the man, not the monument, muſt move, if he desires to know its essential part, the presbytery. In this respeĉt the early connecĉtion between ship- and church-building does not appear. We have seen the evolution from one maſt, as in the ship, to four and twelve, and only in the laſt ſtage to numerous maſts. It is only then that the adaptation to the Roman basilica was complete. The outside of the church which sometimes suggeſted a ship with rigging underwent no great change, but the interior received new proportions not before found in halls and temples. This marked the transition from the broad to the long church.

A typical feature of the ornament of the Viking period is the contraſt between the smooth and rough surface in pierced work, especially in the ſtrap motive and the composition in several planes. A reference to my *Altai-Iran*, etc., will show that these are the formal values also of North Asiatic art at this time or earlier. Organized ſtudy of these queſtions is called for, as they are among the moſt intereſting problems met with in this new direĉtion taken by art-hiſtory. It would not surprise me if here were also to be found, beginning, as we apparently muſt, with the Indo-Aryan movement, the explanation of the preference of the northern peoples for the colours red and yellow.

5. *Content.*—Ship-architeĉture is regarded as a purely induſtrial art, which can hardly be the expression of the soul or the individuality of the builder or architeĉt-designer of the ship. But the artiſt in Viking times is not to be thought of as an individual, as would be the case to-day : he may be

merely the expression of his geographical situation, his local raw material, or the national temperament. It will be agreed, I think, that the Norwegian grave-ships, especially the Oseberg ship, are, like the mast-churches, a group of monuments with an expressiveness of their own, behind which lies the artistic outlook of the North Sea peoples. It is a creative art, in our view, since we now realize that this art of shipbuilding and ornament was precisely that which might find expression in temples, halls, and ultimately, churches. An impressive effect of contrast is obtained between the austere structure of shipbuilding and the rich ornament.

We noted earlier, in considering the outward representation of spiritual states in art, the example of Laocoon, the movements of the body represented the state of mind. To me this represents the inner meaning, which may also be seen in nature. At the same time, the content or expression of the artist's soul is not manifold but single. If the artist has not the human figure by which he may express himself, can he not use lines and colours? Would that necessarily be primitive art? In the art of the Oseberg ship and its furniture there is a striking balance of static and dynamic elements. It would appear that monumental art in wood is a better indication of the artistic values of northern art than the trifling objects in bronze and other metal-work studied by Salin in his great book on northern animal ornament.

Again we recall the massive block churches of Eastern, and the lighter framework of Western Europe, which belong to other provinces of art. Here other artistic values are present. We now require a knowledge of the third group— North European wooden art in mast and stave-work. Then only will a new history of art be possible in which the evolution of art may begin, not from the South but from the North, and the personalities of the northern peoples, by studying the influence of church, court, and education of stone building and the introduction of the human figure.

III. Importance from the Point of View of Evolution.— In the title of my book on Asia Minor I describe it as a new country for the purposes of art-history. These wooden monuments, too, which I have collected for the first time, in view of their important bearing on art-history constitute such a new country, a new country for northern art as Asia Minor was for eastern. My great hope is now to discover behind the Oseberg ship a wide field of research, as I once found in Asia Minor, where the titles of my books, *Mschatta*, *Amida*, *Altai-Iran*, and *Armenia* indicate my general course.

It will be well for us to review, in relation to North European or pre-Romanesque art, the subjects of each of the foregoing chapters. In the first, we dealt with the pre-Romanesque church of the Croatians, monuments [1] with rich interlaced band ornament on stone of the period that we are studying ranging from the seventh to the eleventh century. In the second chapter, on wood architecture in Eastern Europe, it was necessary to deduce by a process of reasoning the earlier types from the innumerable wooden churches. The third chapter dealt with half-timber churches in Western Europe. In the fourth chapter we studied the mast-churches of Norway, and found another field of art, which, as we saw, was not an imitation of the southern stone basilicas, but another art-stream, that of the North Sea, in which the leading art was once shipbuilding. The present chapter illustrates some monuments created by this art.

1. *Constant Elements in Northern Art.*—We are too apt to regard the North as an area receiving its art wholesale from the South. If we remember that, in addition to Western and Eastern Europe, both of which may have had some connection with the South at all periods, and in Christian times with Rome or Byzantium, there is a third and self-sufficient culture-circle not so nearly related to the South as the other parts of Europe, we shall view in their true light the maritime regions of Northern Europe, namely the countries of the North and the Baltic Seas. To the north lie the Arctic regions; immediately to the south, the Celtic, German, and Slavonic countries. Thus there is a rich prospect for our future investigations in the North of Europe, to say nothing of Asia. It would seem that every part has its constant elements up to the time when our art-historians begin to look northwards.

At the present we are only concerned with estimating the position of Northern European, in particular Norwegian, art, the resources of this area in raw materials, and, last but not least, what these Teutonic peoples have to teach us of fundamental artistic values in the history of art. Whether the prehistorians, the ethnologists, or the anthropologists have given us a clear picture of the forces of evolution in the art-history of the North cannot be discussed in this chapter; but at least we may say that no hard-and-fast line must be drawn between

[1] Round, square, and small single-aisled churches with vaults, and furniture.

primitive art and high art in the manner of earlier art-historians. We must enter upon a systematic appraisement of artistic values, by which alone we shall be able not only to deal with one subject chronologically, but to present it as valuable raw material for the spiritual direction of our lives and a system for the natural evolution of art in the future in connection with evolutional forces.

In these five chapters our investigations lead us round Western Europe with its supposed centres in Italy, France, and the Rhine, where the later European art following on that of Greece and Rome reached its highest point of evolution in the monumental stone styles known to us as Romanesque, Gothic, etc. But these western countries also possessed wood architecture. It was already known to Vitruvius as different from that of the East, framework instead of blockwork. We may add that it is without true vaulting, having built-up roofs and ceilings with rafters. The early Christian basilica type was more readily accepted there than in the East, since this Hellenistic basilica had also roofs and ceilings with rafters. The difference consisted only in the raw materials of the walls, the early Christian basilica being built with brick and stone, while in the western countries of the European North, when they did not use freestone but wooden framework, they filled in the walls with various materials, such as clay, twisted work, etc. The origin of the Western European system of vaulting is a highly interesting question, in which, as we said in the fourth chapter, mast-building played an important part.

In these chapters we have dealt only with pre-Romanesque art and wood architecture. It is beyond the scope of our present work to discuss the evolution of the Romanesque and Gothic styles in relation to wood architecture of Western Europe (cf. my *Der Norden in der bildenden Kunst Westeuropas*).

It is surely our duty to show some interest in everything relating to early North European or pre-Romanesque art, and to view the rich prospect opened up in the various shapes and techniques of wood architecture, the unlimited richness of the ornament on the monuments of woodwork, old furniture, ships, churches, which hitherto has only been known to us in stone, bronze, and iron.

The wood monuments call attention to the questions of the flora and fauna of their countries of origin. The oak is not to be looked for further north than 60 degrees, nor the reindeer south of another line, constant factors governing the northern art of Europe and Asia. These points I dealt with in *Altai-Iran,* etc. Here it will be sufficient to recall the existence of three areas in which wooden architecture is found—those with block, frame, and mast-work respectively.

2. *The Influence of the Court, the Church, and Education.*—The course pursued by the art-histories, large and small, is a familiar one. In such matters I am a heretic. I consider that we northern peoples have laid too much stress on outside influences, paying too little attention to the force of evolution in the North itself. From my *Origin of Christian Church Art* it is clear how I should write the history of the great periods of art known to us as Romanesque, Gothic, Renaissance, etc. Then, however, I had not written my studies of the early northern church art and wood architecture in Europe. It is only now that I could write a history of art in Europe from about 1050, when the autocratic power of the church, the monasteries, and the court, and the influence of education, had discarded wood architecture in the North.

3. *The Southern Movement.*—About 1050 a new situation arose. The constant elements of the North took a second place. The art which had up to that time been the outcome of the free play of native instincts and artistic values inherent in the peoples was made subordinate to representation in many forms. It took centuries for the northern temperament to come to a certain compromise with the essential character of southern art, which only came with the Gothic art abhorred by Giorgio Vasari and the Italian historians of the new Western European art. What has been the position of the North in art since that time?

Modern art is unconsciously in search of rules which sometimes have a close resemblance to the principles of the lost northern art. It may be that in the course of these chapters readers have found it necessary to expand for themselves the suggestions made in them, as is the case in modern expressionist art. I discussed this curious point in the second edition of my book, *The Fine Arts of To-day* (Vienna, 1923). It seems to be the sign of a general though unconscious tendency, often capricious in its operation, to repudiate in present-day art the principles of the old southern movement. This movement might awake to a clearer consciousness if artists were to make a serious study of the ancient monuments of the North.

Woodwork in the North is older than monumental building in stone and brick. It was in a flourishing state when Rome and, later, the Roman Church, introduced southern stone architecture into the North.   We found in the early wooden ships and churches qualities which called forth our admiration. Nor must it be forgotten that wooden architecture, which did not suddenly come to an end but still survives, must have had some bearing on the art of the Middle Ages.   It reached its zenith in the centuries preceding the Christian period.   To understand the position of the North in the evolution of art, we must begin with the study of wooden architecture and ornament.

CONCLUSION.

I⊤ is my earnest hope that the five chapters that comprise this volume will have conveyed some impression to their reader of this new field open to students of art : the ancient art of Northern Europe, Teutonic and Slavonic. It may be asked whether this art has merely an academic interest for the pre-historic archæologist or ethnologist; whether, that is to say, the historian of art can afford to leave it out of account, or whether he is bound to treat it as an important and vital stage in the history of art. Has it no connection with what we are taught to call " European " art—that is to say, first and foremost the Greek and Roman, and later the Christian styles of the Middle Ages—or was the old North European art-stream cut off entirely with the advent of the Roman and, later, the Christian ages ?

I believe that the foregoing chapters make it clear that what I call North European Church Art is closely related to this ancient timber building and ornament of the North. The Romanesque and Gothic styles, like the Greek temple, cannot be understood if we consider only the southern stone move-ment and the traditions of Mediterranean art. With this statement I return to what I said in my introduction : a wider outlook is required by the present-day scientific inquirer into the arts than that of the traditional " historian." He cannot accept a West European art that has for the sole factor in its evolution the influence of the Mediterranean peoples, and is known only by stone monuments built directly under this influence. He must also know something of the primitive inhabitants of these lands, the " barbarians," and must allow not only for the existence in Europe of the Middle Zone, but for that of the Northern Zone as well, with its in many ways more independent native art.

This is a phrase to which I feel that some exception may be taken, but I hope that in the foregoing pages I have conveyed an impression of what I mean by it in writing of the European North. In completing this book now after

(165)

a lapse of four years (the original lectures were first delivered in the autumn of 1924), it seems to me necessary to add a few words on the Middle or Mediterranean Zone and its relations with the North.　It is stated in the introduction that wood was the material characteristic of Northern Europe, as leather, the raw materials of the tent, and unburnt brick were typical of the Asiatic North.　A stream of influence from each of these arts worked continuously on the Middle Zone which originally (as we can judge from India and the Mediterranean) was influenced in the main by the geographical South.　It seems that the spiritual identity of the Middle Zone,—in any case, so far as the influences of the court, church, and of education are concerned—originated in the migration of northern peoples to Egypt, Mesopotamia, and the southerly peninsulas of Europe and Asia.　They subdued the indigenous populations and took the power into their own hands.　From this we can understand the recurrence of traces of northern art throughout the Tropic of Cancer, varying in frequency according to their proximity to the geographical North.　Iranian art (I do not speak here of the Achamanidian and Sassanian court art in Persia) never evolved for itself a pure representational art, whilst Greek art, so far as representation is concerned, excelled particularly in the human figure.

The art of the Middle Zone thus appears to me to result from a number of conflicting influences.　Perhaps the reader will now understand better what I mean when I speak of the independence of the native art of the North.　I am speaking, of course, of the period up to about 1050, before the actual establishment of relations took place with Asia, and particularly Iran.

It appears to me that discussions such as those on which we have been engaged have a real importance for present-day education.　In the first place, there is the system of research the reader will find underlying all my deductions. This method of describing monuments, of determining essential characteristics, and of explaining their evolutional significance, has, I feel, an importance in scientific research apart from and in addition to art-history.　It is, in my opinion, only by this method that we can embrace clearly the whole field of vision, and its adoption in the investigation of the fine arts, to which it is so particularly well suited, would seem to me of inestimable value in the sphere of education generally.　This is not the place for a discussion of this very interesting question ;

but I should like again to emphasize the educational value of my theory that instead of accepting, as we have been taught, a single genealogical tree of art in the Mediterranean area from the beginning of what we call history to the present day, there exist actually three such trees related respectively to the three geographical zones I have defined, the intermediate or Middle being, perhaps, the latest, on which are grafted those of the North and South.   Thus the history of art assumes a new and wider horizon, one which might perhaps be adopted with benefit in the study of many other branches of human activity.   We believe our knowledge to be great already, but a survey of the monuments of art of some ten thousand years shows the experienced investigator how lamentably small it is.   Art-historians and archæologists must begin to devote their attention not only to what survives to the present day in stone, bronze, and iron, but, at the same time, to the study of those objects which, being of perishable materials, are for the most part lost to us.   Thus we shall avoid the blind alley into which we are led in the present state of education and research, and we shall face the facts instead of relying on arguments deduced from a combination of philology and history.   At present the two are arbitrarily associated; but if we take a broader view, and consider the essential character of the monuments and their relation to the various stages of evolution, I think that education and research will take on a new lease of life.

INDEX TO TEXT AND ILLUSTRATIONS.

(The figures in heavy black type refer to the page numbers of Textual illustrations.)

Roofs, pyramidal, 57, 134 ; raftered, 91.
Rouen, Aîtres de S. Maclou, 81, Plate
XXIII. ; Palais de Justice, 93.
Rügen, 64.
Rumania, 30, 53.
Ruovesi, cruciform church at, 70 ; plan,
71 ; exterior, Plate XIX.
Rushton Spencer, church at, 83.
Russia, 42, 46, 57.
Ruthwell, 7.

Saloinen, church at, 50 ; plan and
section, 50 ; block pillars at, 62,
Plate XIV.
Salona, S. Maria's, 22.
Salzburg, 102, 104, Plate XXXVI.
Scandinavia, 15, 37, 93 ; Royal Tombs
of, 145-64. See under names of
countries.
Schleswig, plan of a church in, 30, 32.
Scotland, 84 note, 87.
Sedlarica, church at, 52, 53, Plate X.
Seeland, church plans, 31.
Serbia, 30, 42, 49.
Serpents, depicted in art. 151, Plate L.
Shenfield, church at, 96 ; plan, 96 ;
interior, Plate XXXII.
Shipbuilding, influence of, 15, 126, 127,
134, 136, 139, 140, 142 ; essential
character of, during Viking period,
154 ; technique of, 156 ff., 157,
Plate XLV.
Siddington, church at, 83, Plate XXVII.
Silesia, 48.
Slavonic influences. See names of
countries.
Sledges, from Oseberg ship, 146, Plates
XLVIII. and XLIX.; ornament on,
152, Plates XLIX., L., LI.
Smograu, 65.
Sodankyle, church roof at, 54.
Somerset, 58, 94, 97, 99.
Spain, 9, 24, 25, 27, 29, 32, 33, 34, 35,
37, 111, 138.
Spalato, 10 ; details and plan of S.
Martin's, 11 ; stone screen, Plate
I. ; 23 ; S. Nicola, 18, plan 18 ;
S. Eufemia, 19, plan 20 ; the
" Prince " relief, 42, 43, Plate VIII.;
Cathedral, S. Door, Plate XLV.
Split. See Spalato.
Square buildings, 27, 44, 64.
Squinches, 15, 16, 16 ; 32, 43, 46, 67.
Staffordshire, 83.
Starston, roof of church, 109.
Statues, many-headed, 65.
Stave-work, defined, 48 ; 116.
Stein, Sir Aurel, 126.
Stona, 21.
Stone, in building, 26, 27, 29, 111.
Storbeck, church and plan at, 80, 81.
Stow Bardolf, church roof, 92, 93.
Stud-work, 89.
Stupovi, 22.
Sumpertus, 36.

Svantevit, area of temple at, 63, 64.
Sweden, 29, 138 ; boat-graves, 145.
Synagogues, 124.
Szathmar, church at, 55, 57 ; plan,
section and elevation, 56, Plate XI.:
103.
Syria, 114.

Taraz, church at, 57, Plate XIII.
Tombs, royal, in Scandinavia, 145-66.
Torpe, church at, 126, Plate XLIII.
Traù. See Trogir.
Trogir, S. Barbara, 19 ; plan and
section, Plate III. ; lintels, 23.

Ukraine, 46, 53, 57.
Upsala, 145.
Urnes, church at, 117, 118, 121, 122, 124,
126, 135, 137 ; plan, 122 ; interior
at N.E. corner, Plate XLI. ; interior, Plate XLII. ; angular masts,
122, Plate XL. ; ornamentation,
122, 123, Plate XLIV.

Vaulting, early, 27 ; in churches, 38, 114.
Vaulting, wood and, 49 ; tunnel vault,
82, 92.
Velike Karlovice, church at, 71 ; plan
and exterior, Plate XIX.
Velike Mlako, S. Barbara, 51, 52 ; plan
and section, 53, Plate X.
Vendel, cemetery at, 145.
Venice, 23.
Vienna, 101, 102, 103, 104, Plate
XXXVI.
Vikings, 136, 139, 144, 159.
Vis. See Lissa.
Visigoths, influence of, 24, 25, 29, 37,
138.
Vitruvius, 105.
Vogelsberg, church, 93, Plate XXX.

Wales, 94, 141.
Walls, 88.
Warburton, church at, 82, 96, Plate
XXIV.
Warndon, church at, 89, Plate XXVIII.
Wernigerode, 95.
Westanfjerd, church and plan, 70.
Western Europe, half-timber churches
in, 77-115.
Whitmore, 83.
Windows, 16, 126, 135.
Wisby Church plan, 31.
Wood, in building, 8, 26, 27 ; genera
use of, in W. Europe, 46 ff. ; place
in evolution of art, 72, 73 ; of E.
and W. Europe, compared, 77 ;
technique, 47, 60, 64, 69, 90, 91,
101, 124, 125, 126, 127, 139, 140.
See also Shipbuilding.
Worcestershire, 89.
Wulfsahl, church at, 81, Plate XXIII.
Wyschenka Welyka, church at, 68, 69,
Plate XVI.